A Woman's Guide to Buying a Car with Confidence and Street Smarts

Don't Let These High Heels Fool You

Copyright © 2015 by Cathy Droz

All rights reserved. No part of this publication may be reproduced, distributed, or transmitted in any form or by any means, including photocopying, recording, or other electronic or mechanical methods, without the prior written permission of the publisher, except in the case of brief quotations embodied in critical reviews and certain other non-commercial uses permitted by copyright law. For permission requests, write to the publisher, addressed "Attention: Permissions Coordinator," at the address below.

Two for the RoadPublishing
Email: info@HERcertified.com
HERcertified.com

Quantity sales. Special discounts are available on quantity purchases by corporations, associations, and others. For details, contact the publisher at the address above.

Printed in the United States of America

Disclaimer / Publisher's Note
The advice in this book has been compiled over a 20 year association with the automotive industry, and includes both personal experience and research that is true and current as this book goes to print. Neither the publisher nor author accepts legal responsibility or liability for any possible errors or omissions contained herein. The purpose of this book is to impart knowledge that will assist readers in negotiating the car-buying process to a successful outcome, but should not be considered a substitute for legal or financial advice.

ISBN: 978-0-9963898-0-8

A Woman's Guide to Buying a Car with Confidence and Street Smarts

Don't Let These High Heels Fool You

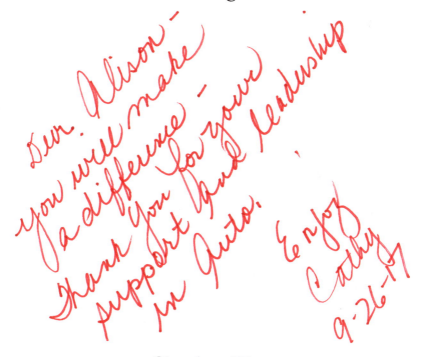

Cathy Droz

Dedication

A special thanks to my mom and dad, Vinny and Ruth Hoffmann, for allowing me to be raised a free spirit, exposing me to life's challenges and letting me make my own choices. You taught me to be open and honest and fight for what I believed in. You encouraged me to always be comfortable with the girl I was and the woman I would become.

Contents

Introduction	1
Chapter 1: My Story	9
Chapter 2: Pre-Purchase Research	21
Chapter 3: Choosing the Right Dealership	47
Chapter 4: Test Drive	57
Chapter 5: To Trade or Not to Trade	71
Chapter 6: Negotiating	83
Chapter 7: The Finance Department	89
Chapter 8: The Drive Away	113
Chapter 9: Service	119
Chapter 10: Final Thoughts	131
About the Author	137
Acknowledgments	139
He Said, She Said ~ What People Are Saying	143
Notes	146

Introduction

I wrote this book for the everyday woman. Whether you are fresh out of school, commuting to your first job, starting a family, a stay-at-home mom, self-employed, retired, divorced, single, widowed or hold a Ph.D. in economics, you will find this guide easy to read and fun to execute. Although this book title says "A Woman's Guide to Buying a Car..." this book will help men as well. We sometimes assume that men know how to buy a car and will often drag one with us to purchase a vehicle, but they too can be intimidated by the process. They just may not admit it.

If you've ever felt scared, unprepared, or even angry when you've walked into a dealership to buy a car or get service, perhaps all you need is a fuller understanding of the buying and selling process – from the buyer's perspective and the dealer's perspective – because *knowledge is power*.

The stories and instructions I have compiled will prove to you that being prepared, doing your research, knowing your needs vs. wants and putting your electronic devices to good use will make the experience of buying a new or used car more appealing than a root canal. All of the preparation and research puts you in the right position to save money as well.

I hope to educate, encourage and entertain you. My Story in Chapter 1 lets you know where I'm coming from in terms of my vast experience: I've been successful in male-dominated industries; raised teenagers as a divorced single mom; and thrived without a college education. I opened an ad agency with $500 and made six figures my second year in business.

I've always believed that book knowledge and street smarts could meet in the middle to form their own category for success. Some say I have an edge to me because I was brought up in New York. They feel that I can negotiate better because I put my humor and sassy attitude to work for me. But that hasn't always been the case. "Don't let these high heels fool you" is a phrase I used often in my life. The High Heels reference is a metaphor about self-confidence, about standing up (in flats or heels) for what you believe is right and fair.

This book is laid out so you get to know me a little better right from the beginning. In Chapter 1: My Story, I'll introduce you to a shy 10-year-old Cathy, proudly learning the secret handshake of car-buying with Dad, my best teacher ever. Then I'll quickly run

INTRODUCTION

through decades of my connection to the automotive industry as, among other things, the owner of an automotive ad agency, freelance automotive journalist, and test driver of over 500 new cars. But after that, this book is all business, teaching you my recommended steps to successful car-buying and service department experiences.

My goal is also to educate businesses to create an environment where every customer feels comfortable through our **HER Certified**™ guidelines. When you see the **HER Certified**™ seal you will know that these companies have gone through an education process, and embraced the customer service requirements we've set for their industry, namely Honesty, Excellence and Respect.

I want to build confidence in women at a very young age and mentor women through my book, website, newsletters, training programs and speaking engagements. My hope is that every woman who reads this book will pass it on to another woman. This is not just about learning how to buy a car, it's about how to negotiate through life and being able to handle whatever comes your way.

Cathy Droz

Now let's get started with some statistics that should make you, the self-reliant car buyer, feel very powerful and confident…

INTRODUCTION

The Incredible Buying Power of Women in the U.S.

If you have ever felt like you aren't being taken seriously when you are making a major purchase for yourself or your family, please know this – retailers ignore you at their peril. From the big box stores to your local auto dealers and everything in between, retailers need women! Just consider the following:

Women are earning, spending, and influencing spending at a greater rate than ever before. In fact, women account for $7 trillion in consumer and business spending in the United States. Over the next decade, they will control two-thirds of consumer wealth. Women make or influence 85% of purchasing decisions and purchase over 50% of traditional male products, including automobiles.

An interesting statistic is that 92% of women say that advertisers don't understand them. The companies say they want to attract the woman buyer, but they don't think past the pink water bottle or a mini-van ad showing a woman loading four kids into it. It's high time that retailers and advertisers acknowledge the inherent differences in the way men and women shop for big-ticket items. For when it comes to spending money, men and women really are from two different planets!

For automotive and other retailers to start appealing to the female market, they should pay attention to these statistics about female consumers:

- Women own 40% of all American private businesses
- Senior women, age 50+, have a combined net worth of $19 trillion!
- 51% of US private wealth is controlled by women
- Women account for over 50% of all stock ownership in the US
- Women control more than 60% of all personal wealth in the US
- Women make 80% of healthcare decisions and 68% of new car purchase decisions
- 75% of women have identified themselves as the primary shoppers for their households
- 50% of women say they want more green choices, including automobiles
- 37% more women are committed to brands that embrace the environment
- Women buy more than half of the new cars in the US and influence over 80% of all car purchases
- Women request 65% of the service work done at dealerships
- Women spend over $200 billion on new cars and mechanical servicing of vehicles each year
- In 47 of the 50 largest US metro areas, single, childless women earn MORE than their male counterparts!
- Moms represent a $2.4 trillion market
- Mommy bloggers influence car purchases and 14% boycott products they don't like

INTRODUCTION

As if all of this information isn't astounding enough, just consider that the AVERAGE woman spends an incredible $54,000 on shoes during the course of her lifetime... now THAT's buying power!

> *Sources: TheNextWeb.com; She-economy.com; StartUpNation.com; Inc.com; GirlPowerMarketing.com; Forbes.com;* TIME; *Nolo.com*

Give a girl the right shoes and she can conquer the world.
~ Marilyn Monroe

Cathy with Dad, Mom and Grandma – Queens, New York

Cathy's brother, Bob Hoffmann, with one of the cars that started it all

Chapter 1

My Story

A little about Cathy today...

Cathy has spent over twenty years in the automotive industry focusing on the fair treatment of women, both in sales and customer service. She is a recognized automotive journalist, radio personality and marketing specialist for businesses and celebrities alike. Her full-service auto ad agency managed million dollar ad budgets and instituted the first Latino auto buying division for nine auto dealers. Her skills as a speaker and sense of humor when running sales meetings focused on how to treat women during the selling process. Her unique events and forward-thinking displays in dealerships, all designed to appeal to women, made her the go-to person for improving women's experiences in the automotive world.

- *She has written, directed, and produced over 200 television and radio commercials and has test driven over 500 cars and is published in magazines, newspapers, television, radio, and on the internet.*
- *Her long-running radio show "Two for the Road USA" was an industry classic, including interviews with some of the most influential automotive men and women of our time.*
- *Cathy's goals are to inspire women to make good choices in automotive purchases, but most of all to have fun in the process.*

How it all started…

As a shy ten-year-old growing up in Queens, New York, I had the fun experience, or chore, of going with my father Vinny to purchase a new car every year. Mom and Dad would each purchase new vehicles every two years on alternating schedules, as well as trading in the old ones, making the trips to dealerships an annual event.

In the 1950's and 60's, most men went alone to buy a car, but my dad liked to take Mom along so she could give the final approval on the color. After several years of my mother being embarrassed by my father's haggling and New York kind of attitude, she said, "Please take Cathy with you next time." I was already the designated one to go to church with him on Sundays; I would now also be accompanying him to auto dealerships. This is what started my annual venture into car buying.

Little did I know that my first experiences at car dealerships would be so enlightening and interesting. I remember my father telling me at the dealership door before we went in, "Don't say a word; I'll do all the talking." Really, I was ten, what would I have to say? "Does this car come with positraction and a cigarette lighter?" I could barely get my saddle shoes off after school, much less discuss cars.

My dad would hold his head high and walk in the dealership like he owned it, and then would immediately walk over to a car and start opening doors and popping the hood. I never understood why he did this because he knew nothing about cars or how they worked. When the salesman approached, my dad put his hand out and introduced himself first, with a very firm handshake. Then Dad would say (depending on the year) "I am interested in such and such" and we would walk over to one of the beauties on the showroom floor. I just stood there and watched the interaction, but was always drawn closer to the open doors by the smell of leather, or in those days, the plastic that covered all the seats.

It wasn't long before we all sat down at the salesman's desk, which was actually on the showroom floor. My dad had a lined pad and beautiful fountain pen with him so he could take notes. Dad would ask for things on the car that I thought only rich people had, like air conditioning, power brakes, power windows and FM radio. Next to each option, he would jot down the price the salesman quoted. I don't remember us getting any of that on other cars, but I did what I was told. I didn't talk; I just played with the pen set on the salesman's desk. All of a sudden, we were ready to go and Dad asked for the man's business card. I was disappointed because I wanted to test drive the car.

Once we got in our car, Dad would turn over the business card and write down the options he had scribbled on his pad and next to it a price. The price was not the same as he was quoted, it was less. Not only that, my dad's handwriting all of a sudden went from Catholic school penmanship to public school scribble. I asked him "What are you doing?" All my Dad said was "watch and learn." I knew I was in for a long night. My mother fed us very early that evening and from the look on her face, I was surprised she didn't pack me an overnight bag. Visiting three dealerships in one evening was the goal.

Dealership number two, just ten minutes from the first, turned out to be very much the same, only this time after Dad copied down the options and prices he said to the salesman, "You must be kidding, your competition up the street will give me the car for X amount of dollars." He showed the salesman the prices on another man's business card. The salesman shook his head in disbelief and said, "Vinny, I can't match it, but I can go down a little on my quote."

Was this the same man that I went to church with every

Sunday, whose sister was a nun, who sent me to parochial school and went to confession? Is this the same man who told me never to lie, cheat or have sex before marriage? Yes it was, and since I was told not to speak, I just looked away. Dad told the salesman, "Well, that is a little better, but let me get back to you. May I have your business card?" Funny, I thought, when I go with Mom to the grocery store she doesn't negotiate the price of her grocery bill or the crackers in aisle 6. Why can my father do this?

We got in the car and again Dad took the numbers off his pad and put them even lower on the back of this man's card. Now his handwriting was even worse, like my family doctor's when giving a prescription for amoxicillin.

At the third and final dealership my father repeated the same drill, and this time the salesman said "I really can't do it Vinny; our competition is selling too low, we can't match or go lower." My dad laughed and said "Okay, leave out the air conditioning and the power windows, take my trade for X amount of dollars and I will pay cash; here it is, where do I sign?" The salesman wanted the sale so badly that he agreed without even thinking it out. My dad wound up getting the car he wanted all along, less the options, and made money on his trade.

We drove home in a brand new car and Dad was so excited and proud we stopped for ice cream (which became a tradition), and I was finally able to talk. In those days, my dad said that car dealerships padded the pricing of their cars with thousands of dollars, and that they expected and enjoyed the negotiating process. He told me that the most important thing was that we got the car we wanted and the salesman made enough money to be a good provider for his family. That made more sense in later years as my dad would always confirm with the salesman at the end of the deal, "Is there enough commission in this for you?" When the salesman said yes, Dad was satisfied.

The car buying experience continued for me from ages ten to seventeen, and nothing changed except my participation.

Age Ten – Watch, listen, and don't talk. At this age my association with cars consisted mainly of hanging out in the garage with my brother Bob and his friends. Most of my time was spent playing with my Barbies, pretending that Ken was a mechanic, and dressing Barbie in her pink high heels to go for a drive.

Age Eleven – Sit inside all the cars on the showroom floor; which felt the best? Open the trunk. Can you fit some groceries and a sleigh in there?

Age Twelve – Sit in front of the steering wheel; can you touch the pedals okay? Can you turn the radio on without taking your eyes off the road? *"I'm in the showroom Dad, what road?"*

Age Thirteen – Sit in on preparation of all the paperwork and watch that the salesman documents everything the way we discussed. *I am now able to hand the marked up business cards to my father on cue.*

Age Fourteen – Pick the color of the car for my mother that year – yellow with black vinyl roof and white wall tires, black leather interior. *I actually handed the cards to the dealer myself. I learned what a title was and found out which car insurance company was ours. (Mom loved the car and got plenty of whistles from the young guys that year.)*

Age Fifteen – Go two weeks ahead of our annual buying trip with my dad to pick up brochures for a Buick, Chevy, Pontiac and Ford. *I studied the brochures and cut out the cars and options like paper dolls and placed them on cardboard so I could discuss the pros and cons with my family.*

Age Sixteen – Drive to dealerships and do the talking. *I had a junior license, so I drove Dad to the dealerships. I got to introduce myself and shake hands with the salesmen. I did most of the talking and through the process I remember them looking at me and then looking at my father with a smirk on their faces as if they were expecting Candid Camera to appear. I discussed with them what we were looking for and didn't have any business cards with false numbers on them; all I said was, "If you can't meet the price, I will go somewhere else." They met the price.*

Age Seventeen – Buy the family car. *I bought the family car while Dad stood outside the dealership only to come in to sign the papers and make sure they didn't take advantage of me because I was so young… not because I was a woman, that never occurred to him or me. Being a woman was not an issue.*

Today you go to the Internet and you are able to obtain a lot of information. Back then you learned a little differently, but it didn't matter if you were a man, woman, or teenager, you needed to know what you were talking about, what you wanted, and what your budget was.

Why did I never feel taken advantage of? Why did I enjoy buying the family cars after I understood the process could be accomplished without fake numbers on business cards or yelling "I'm outta here?" Because, as I mentioned before, knowledge is power!

Did the confidence I achieved from negotiating for the family car have an immediate effect on me? You bet, as I turned down a leadership scholarship that I earned for college, because I couldn't wait to get out in the working world. At seventeen my dream was to work in Manhattan, and I went for it!

Twenty-four Years Later – Age forty, divorced with three children, no career, and no college education, I opened an ad agency for car dealerships. My office was inside a Chevy dealership, but I implemented marketing for nine franchises. Each time I would go downstairs to the showroom floor for something, I would see the terror in women's eyes, whether they had come in alone or with a man next to them. I would watch salesmen with dollar signs in their eyes overtake the women and make them very uncomfortable.

I used to say "Do high heels make us women look stupid?" The salesmen assumed the female customer didn't have a good job, or maybe the husband, father, or boyfriend was right behind them, so why start the process? "Let's just go tell them they look nice" was their typical way to approach women who were shopping for cars.

I would shake my head in disbelief, and soon started leading the sales meetings on Fridays to set them straight. This is where I would enlighten men on how to treat females coming into the dealership. I would tell them to look women in their eyes, shake their hands, and treat them with respect, just as they would a man.

We had some good policies at that dealership, but now and then on a test drive some salesman would ask a customer out on a date or get a little too close when showing them the turn signal function from their seat. Not cool.

Another Ten Years Later – I remarried my ex-husband. Our three children have given us eight grandchildren and now my mom and dad are ninety-six and ninety-seven respectively. I have test driven more than 500 vehicles for all manufacturers. I report on these test drives via Internet, magazines, television, radio, YouTube, my website, and speaking engagements on cars that fit a person's lifestyle, with my focus on women.

Dealerships employ women in all capacities. Men and women alike are trained in handling customers no matter the gender, religious beliefs, or nationality. Women have become more and more important to auto dealers, and the statistics prove it.

I took my dad to buy his last car about six years ago. It was so sweet to watch him look over my shoulder as I copied down on my pad the things he wanted in his Nissan. I didn't have any business cards to fudge with but I did introduce myself, shook the saleswoman's hand with a firm grip and asked to see the invoice. I know he was proud of me. However, he still checked my paperwork with a fine-toothed comb and questioned me on the color. When all was said and done, I walked away in my high heels and took him for an ice cream, just like we had done so many times before.

Take Aways

1. You never know when an event early in your life can change you, or inspire you to find your life's work, or simply build self-esteem.

2. With knowledge of how the car-buying process works, you can enter a dealership with confidence.

3. When buying a car, many women are interested in the mechanical aspects, including horsepower and handling!

4. Ice cream and a great pair of high heels can make all the difference in the world.

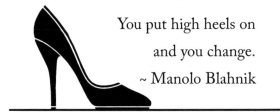

You put high heels on and you change.
~ Manolo Blahnik

You're never too young to get hands on.

Chapter 2

Pre-Purchase Research

Being a Girl Scout was character building, and I will never forget their motto: "Be Prepared." All of the major purchases in your life should be approached the same way. Study and preparation beforehand can get you the best results!

I don't know about you, but I like to search online for the best deal on airline tickets, hotel rates, office furniture, or the perfect pair of shoes at the absolute best price. You might be looking for the best daycare for your child or searching for the first home you are buying on your own. In all of these scenarios you understand the importance of doing your research. The same is true when searching for the ideal auto – you need to sift through a lot of information and separate the glitz from the guts to come up with the facts about all the cars you might consider in your search.

If your life seems too busy to find time for this research, I suggest you use any downtime you have, for example when the kids are sleeping, on your lunch break, or when you are waiting for your child's dance class or football practice to end. With the electronics and technology at your fingertips you can find the time, and with Wi-Fi almost everywhere, this should be no problem.

One thing I still do when auto shopping is create a folder for essential documents. As with any project you take on, rule No.1 should be to stay organized, and that means having everything, all of the important research files you have gathered or printed, in one place, along with forms, business cards and phone numbers. If you think you may trade in your present vehicle, have your title and insurance copies in the folder (or on your electronic device) as well.

Later on you can take this folder or device with you to the dealerships so you are able to produce any material to substantiate your negotiating position. Carrying a folder into the dealership also sends a message to your sales consultant… she's come prepared. I make sure I am. When I was buying cars in the 1960's we didn't have the Internet. I conducted the research on foot, picking up brochures, attending auto shows, watching TV commercials, and most importantly via word of mouth.

Needs vs Wants

I *want* those Manolo Blahnik shoes I saw on "Sex in the City," but I don't *need* them. My budget doesn't allow for $1,300 shoes and my job description at this time doesn't warrant them. Sound familiar?

What can you afford even if your financial situation changes? Take real estate careers for example. One year you're leasing a Mercedes-Benz at $450 a month and the next year the bottom falls out of the industry. Can you still afford $450 a month? Think! What do you need? Is it an SUV, sedan, roadster, truck, van, towing vehicle, hybrid, or electric vehicle? What does your budget allow? I like to utilize "lifestyle matches" when someone asks, "What car should I buy?" Answer the following questions…

- How much time, on average, do you spend in your car weekly?
- Do you have children who need car seats? Might you need car seats in the next year or two?
- Do you have pets and pet carriers that you take in the car with you?
- How about sports equipment? And if you are carpooling, have you considered everyone's gear you need to transport, even if it's a violin case?
- Are you or anyone in your family a caretaker? Allow for mobility equipment.
- Do you require all-wheel drive, front-wheel drive, or rear-wheel drive?
- How important is it for your new car to fit in your garage?
- Are you concerned about the environment and the rising cost of gas? If so, you should be thinking hybrid or electric.

- Did you remember to factor in your fuel costs for the various models? Fuel is a major part of the total cost of owning your vehicle.
- Taxes and License Plates – The tax on your purchase and the cost of your plates will always be based on where you live or where you purchase your vehicle. Check the DMV in your state. For example, some states charge a flat fee for plates and in others it is based on the MSRP of the car. To save money, you might consider buying in a city with a lower tax rate than where you live.

Drive What You Can Afford

Be honest with yourself and determine whether "prestige" factors into your choice of vehicle. I've spoken with many women who are single or recently divorced or widowed who feel they still need to keep up with the status quo of the neighborhood, even if they would be stretching their budget to do so. Drive what you can afford. Be realistic.

I've had women tell me their kids don't want to be seen in the car they selected. "Drop me off a block away," they say. I suggest letting the kids be part of the selection process, while explaining how you arrived at your budget. It's a great lesson in real economics. If they still want to be dropped off a block away, great. You can get to work faster.

How do I calculate my car payment?

Budgeting Tools

For a basic household budget planner go to *BudgetWorksheets.org*. There are also several apps that you can install. You can find a great tool for estimating your car payment at *Autotrader.com/calculators*. For examples of other tools available go to **HerCertified.com** and click on Resources.

And the Research Begins

It's important right from the beginning to know what you can realistically afford, how your credit worthiness factors in, and what insuring your chosen vehicle may cost. Don't rule out your options. Whether you buy or lease or purchase a used car, the buying process is generally the same for all three.

This is the time for you to pull your credit report and check for any inaccurate information. Sometimes we assume our file is correct, but information contained in it can adversely affect your credit score, and therefore your ability to qualify for a loan with a low interest rate. If you check this early in the car-buying process, you will have the time needed to find and correct any errors in your file.

A dealer may want to have you fill out a credit report authorization and have it run off as soon as you decide on a car, or even before that. However, I recommend that you research your credit score on your own and bring the findings with you to the dealership. This way the salesperson can use your score as a guideline when coming up with an approximate interest rate for your car loan. By law, the dealership may not pull your credit file without your authorization. Remember, multiple inquiries will affect your credit score. Later on, the dealership will need your permission to pull your credit file in order to get the final approval on your car loan (we go over this in Chapter 7: Finance). In general, your credit score may vary by a few points, depending from which reporting agency you obtain your file.

There is only so much an auto dealer's finance department can do for you if you have bad credit or errors in your credit report. Therefore, it is imperative that you research what can be done to improve your credit score before you go further in your car quest. More detail on the avenues for the credit challenged will follow, many of which you may not be aware.

How Do I Obtain My Credit Report?

Nationwide Credit Reporting Companies

Each of the nationwide credit reporting companies — Equifax, Experian, and TransUnion — is required to provide you with a free copy of your credit report once every twelve months, if you ask for it. To order, visit AnnualCreditReport.com, or call 1-877-322-8228.

You may order reports from each of the three credit reporting companies at the same time, or you can stagger your requests throughout the year.

Equifax: Equifax.com
Experian: Experian.com
Trans-Union: TransUnion.com

Credit Apps – New Ways to Monitor Your Credit

Currently, one of the best options for checking and monitoring your credit free of charge is CreditKarma.com. Their smartphone app provides a comprehensive look at your credit situation. You receive a 100% free credit score instantly, securely, and safely. Always free, no credit card required. You receive daily notifications of important changes to your credit report. Credit monitoring can help protect your credit. See your real-time transactions and receive notifications about balances, bills, fees and more. Get credit-smart with reviews and advice from more than 20 million Credit Karma members.

What You Need to Know about Your Credit

A score of 640 or less would be considered a sub-prime customer score, so you'd get a poor interest rate. But as long as you were to make your payments on time and keep up with your other expenses, getting the car would benefit your credit score. A 640 credit score should definitely qualify you to lease a $15,000 car. When your credit score is only 599 or less, that's considered "super sub-prime" and signals you need to be concerned about what kind of vehicle you can afford. On the other hand, if you have a credit score of 700 or above, you'll be prime. There won't be much attention paid to your debt ratio (ratio of total debt to total assets) because you'll have the qualified credit.

Effective 2011 any dealership that runs your credit must give you a risk-based pricing sheet. Risk- based pricing allows lenders to charge higher interest rates to consumers who seem less likely to repay their loans in full and on time, and lower interest rates to consumers who seem more likely to repay their loans in full and in a timely manner. If this applies, you should receive an oral, written or electronic notice explaining that your credit has been affected by risk-based pricing. The notice will explain what factors the creditor or lender used in determining the higher interest rate and how to get a free copy of your credit report.

If your credit is not as high as you would like to afford the car you need, you might consider a co-signer.

Do You Need a Co-Signer?

If you have never purchased a vehicle before and you do not have much credit history, you will likely need a co-signer. A co-signer fills out a separate section of the credit application you have filled out, and their credit history and credit score can give your lack of credit a "boost" to get your loan approved. Note: your co-signer needs to have established good credit history or it may have a negative impact on the overall approval of the loan.

A creditor may require that you have a co-signer on the finance contract to make up for any deficiencies in your credit history. If you are a co-signer, you assume equal responsibility for the contract. The account payment history will appear on both the borrower's and co-signer's credit reports. For this reason, use caution if you are asked to co-sign for someone. Co-signers are legally obligated to repay the contract, so make sure you know the terms of the contract and can afford to take on the payments before you agree to co-sign for someone.

Special Programs

Dealers sometimes offer manufacturer-sponsored, low-rate or incentive programs to buyers. The programs may be limited to certain vehicles or may have special requirements, like a larger down payment or shorter contract length (36 or 48 months). These programs might require a strong credit rating; check the manufacturer's site to see if you qualify. Many incentives are for new or even certified vehicles. For example, most manufacturers have a $500 college rebate for people looking for a new car within a few years after they graduate. Other manufacturers have owner's loyalty or competitive bonus cash. Even if you don't have a vehicle yourself, usually as long as someone in your household does, with the same address, you could qualify, even if they aren't trading in.

When you take out an auto loan, you are required to sign a contract that states the terms of that loan. Auto loan terms include many items, for example, the APR or annual percentage rate, the interest rate you pay, the repayment schedule and any associated fees or penalties which may apply. Before you take out any loan you should read through the terms thoroughly. There is a lot of fine print, and if you are not careful, you could end up with an unfavorable interest rate.

Besides the amount of money you plan on putting down, auto loan qualification is usually determined by your income and credit score. If you have great credit but don't earn very much money in a year, the amount lenders might be willing to give you goes down. Likewise, if your credit score is poor, you might get a loan, but only with a higher interest rate. The banks can only finance the vehicle or the vehicle's value. Taxes, plates and fees are not considered part of the vehicle's value. This is why sometimes the banks will ask for a down payment.

There are all kinds of auto loans, from 100% financing loans, same-day loans, to sub-prime credit loans and low APR loans. Look into your options and find out what might match your eligibility. If you fall in to the sub-prime category, your dealer should be able to help you with financing, one way or another, either by waiting until you have a stronger down payment, paying a higher interest rate, or recommending a buy here, pay here loan.

Keep in mind, your credit is your responsibility, not the dealership's or the bank's. The dealership will submit your loan application to the bank or banks it feels best suit your credit situation or type of loan. There are banks that strictly deal with "great" credit scores and banks that deal with "marginal" credit scores (secondary finance institutions). The dealership should work hard to get your loan approved as it is in the best interest of both parties to get your loan accepted.

Shopping for an Auto Loan

- When shopping for an auto loan, rates offered by different lenders vary widely for a number of different reasons. Some lenders are more competitive than others in that they offer lower rates in certain circumstances. Other lenders charge higher rates, but make loans available to borrowers other banks or lenders may not be willing to service. You need to understand how car loan interest rates work and how to find the most competitive rate. Your personal credit score is used as an indicator in determining the likelihood of a default on a car loan.
- If you have great credit you may not need any money down. If your credit is good, fair or poor, you will need some money down. The bank likes to know that you put some of your own money in to the purchase. The general rule of thumb is to have enough money for at least the taxes and plates.

- People with higher credit scores are viewed as more financially responsible and are considered much less of a risk than people who have demonstrated they do not always meet their financial obligations on time. The difference in the interest rate charged to a person with good or excellent credit versus that of a rate charged to a person with bad credit can vary ten points.
- Generally speaking, car loans that have a shorter term usually offer lower interest rates. For example, if you finance a car loan for five or six years, you will almost always end up paying a higher interest rate than you would if you had selected a repayment term of only two or three years. Banks and lenders view longer term car loans to be higher risk than shorter term loans.
- When working with the dealership, don't be afraid to try to negotiate a lower interest rate - especially if you know you have good or excellent credit. If you believe the rate is too high, it may be worth challenging. If negotiations fail, take your car loan request directly to a major bank or local credit union to pursue a better loan interest rate.

Credit Challenged

Just because you have a poor credit history doesn't mean you can't get a car loan. Creditors set their own standards, and not all of them look at your credit history the same way. Some may look only at recent years to evaluate you for credit, and they may grant you a loan if your recent payment habits have improved.

You can rebuild your credit score with on-time payments. It usually takes about six months of on-time or early payments to begin to reverse any negative reports. Once you have re-established your on-time payment reputation, you will find that your credit or FICO score starts to head in a positive direction.

Credit reports and scores are different. While your FICO credit score is generated based on information in your credit report, it's important to understand the difference between the two. Your credit report shows your history of using credit, including the accounts you have (both open and closed), your payment history, credit limits, and amounts owed. Your FICO credit score is generated based on this information, and ranges from a low of 300 to a high of 850.

Getting your report does not hurt your score: You can check your own credit report and score without affecting your FICO credit score. While inquiries by creditors with whom you have applied for credit can lower your score, checking your own score will have no effect on your credit file.

Thirty percent of your credit is based on your debt-to-credit ratio (the amount you owe in proportion to your total credit limit). If you have a high credit limit and you keep your balances low, your debt-to-credit ratio will also be low, so a higher credit limit can help you protect your good credit score. But this is only the case if you continue to keep your balances low.

Debt-to-Credit Example

Let's say that you have a combined available credit limit of $10,000 on all of your active credit card and installment loan accounts. Your balance on these accounts is $2,000, leaving $8,000 of available credit. Your debt-to-credit ratio would be 20%. While each bank or credit union will have their own standards for what constitutes an ideal ratio, a general rule of thumb is that 30% or less is best, with a maximum rate being no higher than 36%. Therefore, the preceding example would be an excellent debt-to-credit ratio.

Credit scores affect more than credit. When it comes to the importance of having good credit, many people think of qualifying for a home mortgage, car loan, or credit card. But the fact is, good credit affects a lot more than applying for a loan. Here are some examples:

- Your credit history affects how much you pay for auto insurance.
- Many employers now pull credit reports on potential employees.
- Landlords could also check your credit before approving a rental application.

Ask Yourself These Questions

Have you paid your bills on time? You can count on payment history to be a significant factor. If your credit report indicates that you have paid bills late, had an account referred to collections, or declared bankruptcy, it will negatively affect your credit score.

Are you maxed out? Many scoring systems evaluate the amount of debt you have compared to your credit limits. If the amount you owe is close to your credit limit, this too will have a negative effect on your score.

How long have you had credit? Generally, scoring systems consider your credit track record. An insufficient credit history may affect your score negatively, but factors like timely payments and low balances can offset that. Have you applied for new credit lately? Many scoring systems consider whether you have applied for credit recently by looking at "inquiries" on your credit report. If you have applied for too many new accounts recently, it could have a negative effect on your score. Every inquiry isn't counted. For example, inquiries by creditors who are monitoring your account or looking at credit reports to make "pre-screened" credit offers are not liabilities.

How many credit accounts do you have and what kinds of accounts are they? Although it is generally considered a plus to have established credit accounts, too many credit card accounts may have a negative effect on your score. In addition, many scoring systems consider the type of credit accounts you have. For example, under some scoring models, loans from finance companies may have a negative effect on your credit score.

I know this is a lot to digest, but in so many ways your credit affects your ability to obtain your new vehicle. This is why I emphasize throughout the book the importance of your credit score.

You will also want to know what finance rates are available from the credit unions, personal or business banks, and other lending institutions. This could be important when you reach the finance department at the dealership, and you need to be ready to compare rates.

Remember that each time you authorize a dealership to look up your credit score when purchasing a new or used car it will show on your credit report. This is a problem when you authorize several dealerships in a row to pull your credit, as it may indicate that you are shopping around for credit. In other words, too many inquiries will result in a lowering of your credit score. That is why, as I mentioned earlier, you want to have your current score either printed or on your device to bring to the dealership. Much further along in the process, when you are ready to "ink the deal," you will need to authorize the finance department to run your credit, but you shouldn't need to at this stage.

Fortunately for you, it is now a federal law that you MUST authorize the pulling of your credit file. This is a wonderful law, as in the past when you comparison shopped, every dealer you visited would make an "inquiry" (pull your credit file), thereby potentially creating several "dings" and lowering your overall credit score without your knowledge.

Now that we have a dose of reality, let's move on with some fun stuff ~ a Needs vs. Wants example.

PRE-PURCHASE RESEARCH

Note: The following is just an example of makes and models. I am not endorsing any manufacturer or brand over another.

I need…
- A vehicle with three rows of seats to fit my family of five
- Enough cargo space for sports equipment
- Room for three large car seats
- Room for a dog crate
- Room for at least two sets of golf clubs
- A payment not to exceed $420 per month
- A fuel-efficient car for my "mostly city" driving

I want…
- A fully equipped GMC Yukon XL 1500 Denali with three rows of seats
- Bose surround sound
- Second row of seats with fold-and-tumble capabilities
- Power rear lift gate
- Two rear DVD entertainment centers
- Captain's chairs with leather seats
- Tow package
- Seating for seven or eight
- Plug-ins for everything technical
- Cup holders for at least six

Really? I want a Bentley and Brad Pitt sitting in the passenger seat. We need to do a reality check and find out which vehicles have what we want, or as close as we can get to it, for a price we can afford. Therefore, I might need a Chrysler Town and Country with my husband in the passenger seat. We might have to give in a little here or there. Brad may need to get the boot, as I doubt he comes cheap.

Consider This

In addition to the Denali you crave as your dream ride, take a look at the new Toyota Highlander with three rows of seats and cloth upholstery with stain resistant fiber.

Think about saving some money on interior options by purchasing dual DVD players you can hook on the back of the driver's seat and passenger seat. These cost about $200 for two, and another $19.99 for the mount, which is a substantial savings over the factory installed options.

Check out the chart below to compare the difference in purchase price on the GMC, Chrysler and Highlander versions. Be sure to also check the overall dimensions to see whether they will all fit in your garage.

Model	Purchase Price
GMC Denali	$68,000
Chrysler Town and Country	$32,000
Toyota Highlander	$31,000

At this point you will want to get a feel for insurance costs as well. So many factors influence the rates you pay to insure your new car, like is it a convertible, sports car, or sub-compact? To obtain ballpark quotes for the various models you are considering go to Insure.com, where you can pull insurance quotes up by state. If you prefer, call your insurance agent for quotes. That way you won't have to give out as much information (driving record, email address. etc.) since your agent already has this on file.

Where Do I Start Searching for My New Car?

It could be you have always been a Honda girl, or a Ford truck gal. If so, you are way ahead of the game here. You already have great brand preference or "loyalty." If not, see what is in your neighborhood and who drives a vehicle you like. Look at television commercials, ads, and reviews on the Internet, social media, or in your local paper. Check out your work place parking lot and copy down the makes and models of cars you like. Ask friends and neighbors if they like their present vehicles. Start taking photos of cars or trucks with your Smartphone (not while driving please).

Don't be turned off by color availability (or lack thereof) or vehicle size until you've researched it more. A fellow journalist of mine is six-foot-six. He told me once he was not going to be able to test drive the Mini Cooper when it came in to the press fleet. Well, guess who fits nicely in a Mini Cooper? Don't count something out until you try it (see Chapter 4: The Test Drive).

Now pick three or four new vehicles you like and start checking out the particulars on various websites like Cars.com, Edmunds.com, KBB.com, and AutoGuide.com. Many of the sites say, "You may also like this model," and then they list a competitor's make and model, which is similar to what you are searching. Sometimes the suggestions are worth looking into and pricing may be more desirable for the same styles and options you need.

The final step in your research is to print out the details on the cars you are interested in (or save it on your device) with the features you need, and the MSRP (Manufacturer's Suggested Retail Price) as listed on the manufacturer's website. Naturally, you would want to add these printouts to your folder. Remember that even though all automotive ads must adhere to the "Truth in Advertising" standards, be sure to read the fine print in all print or website offers to make sure you can qualify for any special pricing.

I have been writing auto reviews for over twelve years with women in mind, so you may find reviews of some of the models you are considering on my website, **HERcertified.com**.

Color: One of the Fun Aspects of Selecting a New Car

Believe it or not, the color of car you choose seems to say a lot about you. Some of us are so color obsessed we will pay extra just to get our new vehicle in our signature color. What does your car color choice say about you? The following *Automotive Color Popularity Report* graphic has some interesting theories on the subject.

Car Color ~ What does it all mean?

Black	Sophisticated, Powerful, Important	Classic
Silver	Innovative, Security-Minded Upscale	Classy
Gray	Dignified, Traditional Mature	Doesn't like to stand out in a crowd
Red	Go-Getter, Confident, Fun	Your car says "Look at me."
White	Fresh, Young, Modern, Honest	Pure
Blue	Practical, Stable, Truthful	Serene
Brown/Beige	Peaceful, Money-Conscious	Self-Assured
Yellow	"Don't Worry, Be Happy" Joy	Positive Attitude
Green	Not a Trend-Setter	Environmentally Conscious
Orange	Money-Conscious Bold Personality	Not Trendy

♦Least purchased color by women: orange
♦Most purchased color by women: white

(Source: 2013 Axalta Automotive Color Popularity Report)

"Cruising" through the Internet

Since at this point you haven't selected a dealership to work with, you may want to stick to the generic sites I listed for basic make and model information. These sites allow you to review details and see pricing without filling in the blanks about YOU. This way, you don't get a sales call during work hours or hockey practice, which might happen if you do research on individual dealer websites. In fact, the manufacturers' sites usually give you more information, including factory rebates and some additional discounts. Be sure to print off or save any applicable incentives on the models you are considering, and put those in your folder as well.

You are trying to gather as much information as possible so when you meet with your dealer you will have everything in order and should know what you want, what you can afford, and what you can expect to pay.

You have now completed research for the three or four vehicles you might want, but you have not visited a dealership yet to start the buying process. This is the Pre-Purchase and Research stage, most of which is spent finding out about you, your needs, and what you can afford.

You should also have found out what your insurance rates will most likely be on each car, based on whether you are military (if you are, thank you for your service), or if you qualify for student discounts, anti-theft protection, green vehicle discount, multiple car discount and maybe even a safe driving discount. Do not forget to ask for your company discount as many corporations are now listed with the manufacturers providing a special employee discount. Every state requires any car you own and drive be insured, and if you finance a car, the bank holding your loan can stipulate the type of insurance you get. If you purchase a sport or luxury model, you may be paying well over $1,000 more a year.

And back to the idea of needs versus wants ... I may not be able to afford a pair of Manolo Blahniks, but I found a similar pair of shoes at Macy's within the Jessica Simpson line that served my needs. I know Jessica Simpson isn't Manolo Blahnik, but I got the shoes I needed and could afford.

Take Aways

1. Go online to get some very important back-up information to substantiate your research: an estimate of the sales price of the car or cars you have chosen, an estimate on the payment, and approximate insurance rates.

2. Create a "wants" vs "needs" inventory and get a clear picture of the car and accessories you REALLY plan to acquire.

3. Take care of your credit score. Avoid multiple inquiries and correct any deficiencies.

4. No matter what the *Car Color* chart indicates, the most important thing is choosing a color you like!

It has always been a dream of mine to create an auto dealership model that is more welcoming to women. Throughout the book you will find my suggestions for the "perfect" dealership experience.

> **IF I OWNED A DEALERSHIP…**
>
> I would set up seminars in the evening or on Saturdays at my dealership. The classes would be open to the public (men and women) and FREE. They would be designed to educate consumers about what they need to know before they purchase a vehicle. The classes would be run by automotive finance, insurance, banking and credit-challenged specialists. An informed consumer is a happy consumer. High quality beverages and food would be provided.

Mama always said you could tell a lot about a person by the kind of shoes they wear.
~ Forrest Gump

Chapter 3

Choosing the Right Dealership

Finding a dealership you are comfortable with, that has all the things you are looking for, is a process much like trying to find the right school for your child. The schools all claim they can give you exactly what you want and the prices for doing so are within a few dollars.

Therefore, wouldn't you want to look for a school close to your home or work? You would interview the teachers, visit a classroom, evaluate the culture, ask to see their credentials, check reviews online, or ask other parents about their experience, right? It should be the same when searching for the right auto dealer.

Reputation and Location

Now that you've decided on the makes and models you'll be considering, you are on your way to having some fun!

First, go to your trusted sources. Check the reputation of the dealer through friends, family and resources like the Better Business Bureau, Yelp.com or Google where you can check not only the dealer's reputation, but their service department ratings and reviews as well.

Second is the location factor. Do you want the dealer to be close to your home or your office? Think about how easy it will be to take your car in for service or warranty work after the sale or how convenient it would be to just drop in to ask a question before or after the sale?

Consumer polls indicate women tend to support dealerships that are involved in the community and nonprofit organizations. If that is important to you, look for links on that dealership's website that list their community partners. You can also check out awards, plaques, and so forth when you visit the dealership.

Just like you would evaluate a school, I suggest asking yourself some questions after a visit to any prospective dealerships. For example, "Did you like how you were greeted?" Most dealers train their staff to greet you once you've stepped onto the property or approach you while you are looking at cars in the lot. Women find that one of the most dreaded parts of car shopping is being approached by sales staff the second you reach the parking space or front door. This is overwhelming and looked upon as unprofessional.

- Meet and Greet – A courteous exchange of welcome, a handshake and quick question such as "How can I help you?" They want to make a good impression, so if they seem to want to get personal it might just be part of building rapport. Here is where the eye contact comes in and they will want to memorize your name or names to use during conversation.

- Qualify – In order to help them understand your needs and wants they should ask you several questions – quality questions. They should be good listeners and do fact finding. Once they know what kind of vehicle you like they should want to know more about your passenger and cargo needs.

- Walk Around/Test Drive – Once you've narrowed it down to a particular car model, the sales associate may want to do a walk-around and then a test drive. This is where they show you all the features and build up the excitement!

- Write Up – After the test drive is when most potential customers take off and the sales associate faces the fact they may not return and they have lost a customer. Here is where they might say "If I can work out the numbers to your satisfaction can we make a deal on the vehicle today?" It doesn't always help close the sale, but the question should not be offensive; it's their job to ask. In order to keep you interested you might be asked if you have a trade.

- Close – The sales associate would like to get some kind of paperwork started on you so a negotiating process can begin and they can help you buy a car and get you out the door in a timely manner. If you have communicated your intentions to purchase that particular vehicle they will want you to come inside the dealership after the test drive.

- Tour and Finance – While paperwork is being done they are to give you a tour of the dealership, especially the service area, where they might set up your first service appointment. They are to escort you to finance.
- Delivery – When you have purchased the car, they will go over the car inside and out and answer any questions before you leave. This is when they tell you to call them any time to answer any questions that come up later as they want you to be happy with your new vehicle.

This is a quick overview of what most auto sales training involves. Even though times have changed in the auto industry, sales training methods have changed very little.

Culture

Do you like the atmosphere or "culture" of the store? This can be as simple as how easy it was to park, how you were greeted, the cleanliness of the store both inside and out, how professionally the staff is dressed. The "culture" (customer service guidelines) is a behavior that is established by the General Manager and/or owner and it is important to understand that a store's tone is established at the top. Even how a phone call or email is handled can be an indication of the culture of the dealership. It is important to understand that you are looking for an auto dealer to help you buy, not sell you!

I can evaluate a dealership rather quickly.

As I approach the door of the dealership and the sales associate says to me, "May I help you today?" and I say "Not right now, but thank you, I'm going inside to look around." I would hope they would say, "Sure, take a look around and if I can answer any of your questions, please let me know. My name is Jason." They may ask you one more question like: "Are you looking to buy or lease, and do you have a trade?" I would say, "I'm not sure yet, Jason, but I will look for you when I have made up my mind." Now I take a mini-tour of the facility, including the service department, ladies room and the waiting area where I can check for children's play area, Wi-Fi, and possible refreshments. You should be able to tell in a few minutes if this is the dealership for you. Call it a "gut" feeling, or woman's intuition. I've walked out of dealerships five minutes after arriving, while in others I wanted to buy a car because they were so accommodating.

Check out the other dealerships on your list throughout the week or the same day, then be ready to go to the dealership you have chosen and interview your sales associate.

Match.com for Your Sales Associate

You've heard of dating sites like Match.com and eHarmony where you are paired up with the man or woman of your dreams based on data you've provided. It might include criteria like enjoying long walks on the beach or gourmet cooking at home, but the matching is based on compatibility. In most cases you write a profile about yourself and what you are looking for in a mate. The same goes for finding the right match for your sales associate. After all, you want to be happy with the person you are going to spend the next two to three hours with.

Many dealerships operate on an "up" system. This system refers to the practice of a rotation of sales associates to take care of, or approach, the next person or family coming into the dealership. I look at it like the bakery or deli department of a supermarket. Take a number, and when your number is called, you're "up." Of course in the dealership world, when you are the "up" you don't get to pick the deli sandwich of your choice.

Once a sales associate approaches a customer coming out of her car or walking in the door, he or she will welcome you to the dealership, extend their hand and introduce themselves. Now, if you are looking for a car and the first person who approaches you considers you their "up," you are not assigned or committed to that person in any way. I bet you thought you were. Read on for one example.

Three years ago when shopping for a car with my daughter's friend, we were approached by a man in his fifties who introduced himself as "Ted, but you can call me Teddy" (finding himself quite funny, Teddy laughed out loud at his statement), then he went on for five minutes with a comic ending, "I'm here for you, kiddo."

My daughter's friend took one look at me and said quietly, "This is why I don't like car shopping."

It was at this point I asked her, "Who would you feel more comfortable working with?" She said "A woman with some experience, maybe the age of my mom." I told Teddy we would get back to him, but we would like to see the sales manager. I had my daughter's friend herself tell the sales manager she would like to work with a woman and preferably more of a mother figure. He called over a saleswoman who fit the description, they chatted for a little bit and from there a relationship and a sale developed. It would have been a shame for this potential customer to have walked out based on her impression of Teddy, because she had done her research and liked the dealership.

If you want to work specifically with a man or a woman, or someone who is technology savvy, or one with 20 years' sales experience, ask to see the sales manager. Ask to be matched with the type of sales associate you prefer, and communicate the type of sales associate for which you would be best suited. The dealership should be happy to do so. Sometimes the general sales manager himself or herself will work with you. Never be hesitant to ask for what you know is best for you.

The auto industry is a very competitive business, and the make and model you want usually has more than one dealership in town. Therefore, you have many options when choosing your dealership and sales professional.

No matter which dealership you choose, remember to come equipped with all of your research, including your comparison pricing and credit report in your folder. Bringing a pen and pad or iPad to take notes is also a good idea.

Take Aways

1. Evaluate the atmosphere and culture of the dealership you are considering. If you don't like the vibe, move on.

2. You are not committed to the first person who approaches you at the dealership. If you don't feel a connection, or establish rapport, ask for someone else to assist you.

3. Having a clear understanding of the standard sales process followed in most dealerships will help you navigate through the system.

IF I OWNED A DEALERSHIP...

- I would have the sales staff inside the dealership and a concierge meeting customers near the door.

- The concierge would do the "meet and greet" and offer the customer a choice of sales consultants from a book or refer to the website's "About Our Staff" with a bio under each photo. The customer would pick their ideal consultant.

- The concierge would provide visitors with refreshments and a short tour of the dealership.

- The ladies rooms would have ambient lighting, liquid soaps, lotion, and hand sanitizer. I like family bathrooms so that men or women can take their children with them. These family bathrooms would include well-stocked changing tables.

- I would create a pet-friendly area near the dealership's service waiting area.

- It would be all about the "customer experience."

Is the dealership you've chosen pet-friendly?

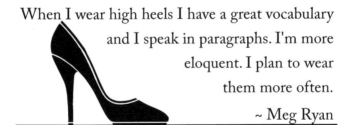

When I wear high heels I have a great vocabulary and I speak in paragraphs. I'm more eloquent. I plan to wear them more often.

~ Meg Ryan

Chapter 4

The Test Drive

As an automotive journalist I've driven over 500 new cars in the past twelve years. At the end of my test drive week (seven days) I report my findings and personal opinion via magazine articles, radio, television, blogs and social media. Yes, I am the envy of many an automotive enthusiast when a new car arrives in my driveway weekly. My neighbors like to drop over on Wednesdays to see what new car, SUV or truck I'm testing. If any of them want to sit inside, check under the hood or trunk, it's fine with me. I've sold many a car for the manufacturers because of my Wednesday driveway deliveries.

I have an extensive checklist I refer to when testing a car for the manufacturers. When you are doing your test drive in the cars or models you are considering, your checklist should be just a shorter version of what I do. My suggested checklists for you are contained in this chapter. Here are some recommendations to assure the best possible assessment of your drive. For more information and samples of auto reviews go to **HERCertified.com**.

First Things First

- You will need to give the dealer your license so they can make a copy for their records. This is for your safety and theirs. Think about it, would you let a stranger drive your car? You can purchase a car without a driver's license but you cannot test drive one.

- Test drive the exact model or models you have discussed with your salesperson. If you are looking to spend $19,000 on a new sedan make sure you are driving that one, not the LX, LE, LS, LT or LTZ model which might be significantly more expensive. Your salesperson can discuss the upgrades with you either during or upon your return from your test drive. Drive the one you would buy.

- Bring a friend to be the designated test drive passenger (they too have a responsibility). Have them take photos or notes so you are free to concentrate on the drive and how the car functions. In fact, your passenger can hold the checklist and pencil in your comments. Don't hesitate to let your sales associate drive too. This way you can evaluate the comfort and amenities from the passenger's perspective.

- Twenty minutes is the average time a dealer allots for each test drive; you may need or want more. This is no problem; just let your associate know in advance.

Before You Leave the Dealership

- Walk around the vehicle with your sales associate. Ask questions about the exterior such as: "Are there any upgrades or new innovative features in this model?" Your salesperson's enthusiasm during this "walk around" may be contagious!

- Does the overall look of the car and the color say "that's me?" Is there another color you feel is more suitable and do they have it in stock? You may love green for your T-shirt but for your car, maybe not! The color you choose, depending on where you live, can have a bearing on your choice. Did you know that in a hot climate, a black car parked outside can be at least 10 degrees hotter inside compared to a white car?

- Is it easy to get in and out of the car? If you are the driver make sure you can effortlessly maneuver yourself in and out. Think about how you are dressed and your footwear. Some outfits and shoes require a little more finesse when entering or exiting a truck or SUV for instance, so keep that in mind.

- Is the upholstery choice cloth or leather? Do you have children who like to eat in the car and possibly fling a sippy cup now and then? Does the leather "breathe"? Will it clean easily?

- Are the seats comfortable? Check the leg room and head room. Maybe you are five-foot-two but your boyfriend is six-foot-six. Find a tall guy at the dealership and ask him to sit in the seat to verify the head room.

- Do the seats adjust to your liking? Remember that the minimum distance between your chest and the steering wheel should be ten inches, but eighteen inches is recommended. Is the head restraint in a good place for you? If not, adjust it for the test drive.

- Are the seat belts comfortable? Ask your friend in the back seat if he or she is comfortable. Are the seatbelts easy to buckle? Ask your associate, if you don't know already, about the placement of the safety air bags and the safety check ratings.

- Check rear view mirror for visibility and ease of adjusting. In addition to the mirrors, check for general visibility in the driver's seat. Are there any "blind spots" that would make you uneasy in changing lanes?

- Check side mirror adjustments. Anything awkward, too big, or too small?

- Are the pedals and the steering wheel in a good placement? If manual transmission, is the gearshift easily accessible?

- Is the dashboard easy to reach without taking your eyes off the road? Are the knobs in a stack in the middle? Do you have a safe reach with your right hand and arm? Push button or touch screen?

- How does the audio system sound? Change channels, check to see where your charger would go, how many USB ports, and if you like, how the vehicle accommodates your iPod.

- Is a navigation system part of your package? Bluetooth for hands free dialing, voice activated commands, OnStar or similar, Sirius or similar?

- How easy is it to get in and out of the back seat? Try the same in and out agility testing as the passenger and driver. Are there grab handles, dry cleaning hooks, rear climate controls, cup holders or even an armrest that has a pass through and more goodies inside the armrest?

- If the car is a convertible, how easy is it to open and close the top? Have the sales associate show you how to operate and then you do it. Test drive with the top up and then down. Too noisy or too much hair blowing?

- How many child safety seats will fit, if that is applicable? If you are planning on having more children or grandchildren, does the back seat accommodate various sizes and makes of child safety seats and like products?

- Is the cargo area ample for your lifestyle? You should have a mental list of the items you might want to transport, vacation with or need for sports and children, or even a wheelchair when needed for aging parents or injured family members.

- If there is an open cargo area, is there a cover? Is there a safe place to store your purse under the rug or in the spare tire well when you are parked for long periods of time?

- Do the back seats fold to increase trunk/cargo space? If you are a skier for instance, can skis fit top to bottom using the pass through spot or along the passenger seat side? If you surf, check the roof to see if racks can be purchased aftermarket to accommodate your board(s).

- Is there a spare tire, an inflator kit, or run-flat tires? Does the vehicle have a Tire Pressure Monitor system?

- Are there tools to fix a flat? A first aid kit? Whether you would fix the flat yourself or get some help, the proper tools are needed. A first aid kit is not standard in all makes, but I suggest having a well-equipped safety kit in your car based on your geographical area, medical needs, climate and driving habits.

You can print this checklist at **HERcertified.com**, *click on Resources.*

Ready for the Pavement

Depending on your lifestyle, or the primary use of the car, request those test driving locations that will give you the best feel for how the car handles. Drive on a busy street with stop and go traffic, then speed up a little for the freeway drive. Now move on to the supermarket or local industrial park to check the ease in parking and backing up. Park between two vehicles and see if the turning radius works for you. Try parallel parking the car on the street, where in many cities that is all you can do. This is basic. Now let's move on to a more detailed checklist.

It is during the test drive with your sales associate that you should be addressing the **Checklist for the Road**. The sales associate is there to assist you and point out certain features and amenities the model car you chose offers. Keep the sound system off so you can hear the sounds of the car internally, externally and also hear the sales associate speaking. The friend you brought with you should be taking note of items and even snapping car selfies so you can concentrate on the road and testing. It's good to be excited about the car but try to control your emotions and not get caught up in the new car smell or be nervous about your budget.

You've done your homework, you know you can afford it ... relax and enjoy the test drive.

Checklist for the Road

- Is the steering wheel comfortable? Is it adjustable? Does it telescope in and out and adjust up and down?

- Evaluate steering and handling at low speeds and high speeds. Do you feel like the road is inside the car with you? Does the car have a stiff feel to it, or do you have considerable movement when steering?

- If manual transmission, do the clutch and gas pedals have an even, smooth flow to them? Are you jerking from a stopped position because the gears aren't meshing or simply because you are inexperienced in the method of smoothly accelerating a stick shift vehicle?

- Is the vehicle's acceleration acceptable to you, or do you find it lacking? Does the vehicle's power meet your requirements? Passing, how is the acceleration? – Passing another car on the freeway as you accelerate should leave you with a feeling of control as this is a safety issue, not a race to the next exit for fun.

- Heater and A/C – Depending on the season, try out the current system needed. In extreme cold climates and equally extreme hot climates car interiors need to be cooled and warmed up quickly. Estimate the time it takes. Are there vents in the rear, and are they controlled by the driver or the passengers? Are the seats cooled and/or heated?

- Check windshield wipers and washer fluid spray. Your new car should come filled with fluids. If you are testing an SUV or crossover or van there may be wipers in the rear as well.

- Check the emergency brake on an incline if possible. If you are on flat ground you need to see how easy or difficult it might be to release the brake.

- Is there a sunglass holder or small mirror above the rearview mirror? I call them backseat monitors. If you have small children you can watch who hit who by looking in the mirror: if you have teens you can see any faces they make when you tell them to turn-off their electronics.

*You can print the Checklist for the Road at **HERcertified.com**, click on Resources.*

Back at the Dealership

When you have returned to the dealership you might want to test another model, or an upgraded level of the car you just drove. Just let them know. If you are not ready to sit down and start the paperwork on the vehicle you drove, just say so. You are not committed; don't feel bad. You need to be totally satisfied and excited about your choice.

I suggest you check out the trunk/cargo area again. Do you need the remote in your hand to open the trunk? From which side of the vehicle do you fill the gas tank and does it open from inside the car, with the remote, or do you access from the outside with the push and open method? Is the tailgate on the SUV hard to open and close (manually or with the push of a button)? How easy is it to get the trunk open with groceries in your arms or holding a child's hand and a package?

Consider your lifestyle at all times when looking to purchase your vehicle.

Dealer Staging Area™

If you are lucky enough to be at a dealership with a staging area, this is when you check out the functionality of your test car. The Dealer

Staging Area™, which I have recommended to certified dealers, is a section on the showroom floor where both lifestyle and unique objects are available. You want to be able to test to see if the car, truck, SUV or van holds certain items or fits specific equipment that is very personal to your life. The area should include things like skis, child safety seats, golf clubs, snowboard, surfboard, filled grocery bags, grass seed bags, and a child's stroller. This way you don't have to take seats out of your car or go home and find out your golf clubs do not fit. This saves time and money and is actually fun.

After Dark

If you did the test drive during the day, I recommend you come back and test drive again at night. The lighting in many cars, both inside and out, can be a surprise the first time you go out at night.

Ambient lighting and colors used for dashboard display could actually freak you out. If you wear contacts or glasses and didn't have them on during the daytime test drive, please put them on for the night test. This may sound silly to you but many a person who said "Oh it will be fine at night" wishes they had gone back to see the little nuances that became a negative after they purchased their new car.

Can We Talk?

Now that you've test-driven during the day and at night and have narrowed your choices down, but don't want to start the paperwork, you should explain to the sales associate that you have a few more dealers to check out. Take a photo of the window sticker and include the VIN number or stock number. This makes it easier when you return for your associate to pull up the car you want to buy. Be true to your word. If you say you will call either way, then do so. Take the associate's business card and call with your decision when you are ready. Please keep in mind, once you leave the dealership, the vehicle you have been testing may be sold to someone else.

Take your checklist for the vehicles you drove, sleep on it or grab a cup of coffee with your test drive partner and see what best fits your lifestyle, budget and excitement level. Many dealers have a 24-hour "try it for a day or weekend" policy. Check with your sales consultant to see if your dealer does. Test drives should be fun. I love the new car smell and when you test drive several cars in a short period of time, you can get addicted to the smell. It's much like trying on several pairs of shoes at the department store… it's habit forming.

Take Aways

1. Test drive the exact make and model in which you are interested. Bring a friend, take photos and bring the checklist in this book with you.

2. Request test drive locations that reflect your day-to-day life – athletic fields, gym, office, school, supermarket, train station.

3. Consider everyone or everything that accompanies you on a typical drive. Do you have enough space? This could be pets, kids with sports equipment, musical instruments or Grandma's walker.

4. If your dealership has a staging area, use it for peace of mind.

5. Ask to take the vehicle home for a day to be sure it is the perfect fit.

IF I OWNED A DEALERSHIP...

- I would have an area designated in my dealership that included many of the items that families keep in their cars and also what the customers would transport for work, hobbies, or sports. If a customer wants to see if their golf clubs will fit in the trunk, but they don't have their clubs with them, then these "staging areas" can supply similar items to check it out right then! Other suggested items are pet carriers, skis, lumber, child safety seats, wheelchairs, and tools.

- I would make a copy of my test drive checklist to give to the customer, and lend them a clipboard for taking notes regarding the test drive, or have their friend take notes during the drive. (See the back of this book for note taking.)

Test drive a car like you test a pair of shoes.
~ Cathy Droz

Chapter 5

To Trade or Not to Trade

To trade or not to trade… that is the question.

One of the first things your sales associate might say to you during their great expedition through your buying habits and personal fact finding is "Do you have a trade?" You might respond with, "Not at this time" or "It depends."

Don't allow your trade to be part of the price of the car. You are negotiating on the vehicle you want to purchase or lease and you don't want the trade to be considered part of the negotiating until you have the agreed upon contract price on the car you want to buy.

Dealers want your business and your trade (even if it's an old vehicle) so they can use it in the negotiations, and possibly resale if it's a fit for their present used car inventory. However, sometimes your trade might go to an auction with other "trade in" vehicles. You shouldn't care where it goes as long as you know what it is worth. It is also the question of making it easy on yourself. Sell them your old car and make payments on the new total you owe. You are right, it is so much easier, just bring your title, hand them the keys and call it a day. I've done it several times. In addition there can be significant tax advantages if you live in a state that reduces your taxable amount by the value of your trade-in (sales tax on the difference law). If you do trade your car, depending on the state you live in, you might only pay sales tax on the difference between the new car sales price and the value of your trade in.

Deciding whether to trade your car in also depends on certain factors. Let's say you are looking to purchase a current Toyota Highlander and you want to trade in your four-year-old Highlander. If you are at a Toyota dealership, you have a better chance of an advantageous trade. Dealing with the same brand, model and dealership is usually the best scenario when it comes to trades. They would probably love a four-year-old Highlander on the lot, as they can most likely sell it at a nice profit. Most dealers agree that any trade under six years of age will sell for more money and thus you will be offered more for your trade. Additionally, a mileage threshold of 10,000 miles per year will favorably impact the value of your trade-in.

Negative Equity – Trade Ins

If you owe more on your vehicle than its market value, you have negative equity in your vehicle. This is a consideration if you plan to use your vehicle as a trade-in. The longer your credit contract, the longer it will be before you have positive equity in the vehicle — that is, before it is worth more than you owe. If you have negative equity, you may need to make a bigger down payment. Or the dealer may offer to include the negative equity in your new finance contract by increasing the amount financed to include the amount you still owe on your current vehicle. This can increase your monthly payments on the new contract in two ways: it adds to the amount financed and increases the finance charge. If you have negative equity in your vehicle, consider paying down the debt before you buy another vehicle. If you use the vehicle for a trade-in, ask how the negative equity affects your new credit obligation. Paying down the debt may be the answer for you, especially if the warranty has expired.

Independent Sale

Don't feel like you can't sell your car by yourself. You can! Here are some helpful hints for getting ready for the sale, preparing the ad, and an example of a car I sold on my own.

Websites such as the NADA (National Automobile Dealers Association) or Kelley Blue Book will give you the value of your car based on make, model, condition, mileage and geographic area.

Before you decide to trade you should acquire values for your car from several sources to determine a more accurate current value. Be sure to print out or save these values and have them in your folder.

You can then go to eBay.com for examples of similar autos for sale or autos.yahoo.com to see the final selling price on your make and model.

Once you've determined what you can ask for your vehicle, make sure it is in the best condition possible. Clean it inside and out, maybe even have it detailed. If you have kept all the maintenance invoices (I suggest you do that), have them in a folder in date order.

Be able to provide an AutoCheck Report or CarFax (minimal cost) that a buyer can take home. This will show your mileage has not been rolled back, the car was never flooded or junked or in a wreck. These are some of the things buyers want to know before they purchase a used car. Having this information shows the prospective buyer you mean business.

If the vehicle you are selling is still under factory warranty or you purchased an extended warranty, and the term is not up, make sure you mention that in the ad. Added value would only increase your profitability. Some warranties transfer over to the new owners, but there are some exceptions so do your research. If you have the Carfax for your vehicle, the manufacturer's warranty is usually disclosed.

Ladies, place your ads without giving any information that might lead someone to your home or office. I suggest you do not post your cell or home number or your personal email address. How will they get in touch with me you ask? I have discussed this subject with law enforcement and they suggest purchasing a pre-paid cell phone. Also, activate a new email at no charge through your email provider with a generic username to use specifically for your car sale. Both of these ideas can be used again in other circumstances when you feel your safety may be at risk.

The National Insurance Crime Bureau (NICB) advises anyone trying to sell a car on Craigslist to follow their very specific guidelines which can be found at Craigslist.org/about/scams. I personally feel their guidelines on "Avoiding Scams" and "Personal Safety" are excellent sources of reference.

Also, do not photograph the vehicle in front of your home or place of business; please keep in mind that the more photos that you have of your vehicle generally reduces the time required to sell your vehicle. I recommend that you have a minimum of sixteen photographs. Again, the best way to maximize the value of your vehicle is with photos, and the more photos the better.

Look at other ads and be creative. Do not lie, but style your ad so the person looking for your car wants it more than any other car.

My favorite way to show a car at its best is to have the car impeccably clean both inside and out, and then place a nice little fragrance under the driver's seat.

If you are a smoker, please let potential buyers know.

I suggest when you need to meet prospective buyers, you do so at a highly public place, preferably at a police station. Ask for their driver's license and take a photo of it and the interested buyer for collateral. Do not test drive with them by yourself. I strongly suggest that you take a friend with you for backup support and a ride home in case you sell the car.

This is my car that I sold in 2014.

You can never be too careful. As you can see, this is why many women just give the dealer their trade in – less hassle. However, I want to see you get every penny you deserve for your trade.

You can put a "for sale" sign on your car and leave it at the local corner (could be ticketed) or simply have a "for sale" sign on your car wherever you go. Make sure you have the price on it so people who can't afford it aren't calling you. But be aware that if you have a for sale sign on your car, it gives people an excuse to walk up and engage you in conversation or ask you to roll down your window.

Add $100 to your budget for advertising your car for sale. This should get you a 'Premier' Internet ad with features such as significant photos, run till it sells, and privacy email. Autotrader.com, carsforsale.com, ebay.com/motors are all automotive websites where you can sell your vehicle.

You could get more than a dealer offers you, but be ready to negotiate. My ads indicate I am firm on the price and I stick to my guns. I know what my car is selling for based on make, model, mileage, year, and the interior and exterior condition, so the price is already where I am comfortable. I would negotiate perhaps 5% off that price if it was the right buyer. Set the lowest price you can accept and don't play games. You don't like pricing games in a dealership, so price it right and stick to your least possible amount that you are willing to take. Let them walk if their offer is unacceptable. There are plenty of buyers out there.

Necessary Documents to Sell Your Car Yourself

You can download a bill of sale form off the Internet called Motor Vehicle Bill of Sale (you can find these forms to download on your state's official motor vehicle site) to fill out for you and your buyer. I also recommend having the buyer sign an "as-is" statement. You can construct the short letter yourself stating both parties agree on the condition and price, you own the vehicle "as is." It will limit your liability if the deal is questioned for some reason later on. Have your title ready to sign over as well.

You may consider doing your final transaction, including the exchange of cash and signing off on the title, at your bank. It is convenient for notarizing and is a safe place to exchange funds and information. You can also immediately deposit the money into your account.

You can see why trading in your vehicle to a dealership can be easier than what I've just described. However, did I mention selling your car on your own can be challenging, profitable, and even fun at the end of the day?

If You Trade Your Vehicle in at the Dealership

Your research has informed you what you can expect for your trade, so when you are negotiating and the sales associate asks, "Do you have a trade?" you can confidently let him or her know that you might be interested. Be clear up front that you know your car's trade-in value. Make sure the sales associate gives you a separate price for the used car. Know what he or she would give you on the trade alone – no bundling and no smoke and mirrors.

Also note that when dealers look at your car to give you an estimate, they do consider year, make, model, mileage and condition; then they walk around and point out areas that are dented, chips in paint, worn tires, sun damage, etc. This is done to justify their pricing. You must keep in mind that the dealer is valuing your car from a perspective of them profitably reselling your car. This comes with certain responsibilities, of which consumer safety is their number one consideration. If it is too costly to bring your car up to the dealer's used car standards, then the dealer will sell your car at auction.

You've researched the worth of your car, and now with the dealer's input you can negotiate the best price for yourself. Be aware, the dealer can look up your car in what is called the dealer Black Book where they have the most up-to-date vehicle data (value) exclusively for dealers. As you can see, there are many variables that determine the value of your vehicle: make, model, mileage, condition, and demand/desirability in the resale world.

Take Aways

1. If you trade your car, depending on where you live, you may only pay the sales tax on the difference between the new car sales price and the value of your trade in. Understanding the value of the trade and the rules of the dance keeps you feeling confident. Don't let "trade or no trade" be a part of the negotiation on price.

2. If you elect not to trade in your old car, selling it can be a great experience if you're prepared. Give the prospective buyer an AutoCheck Report or CarFax to show the mileage has not been rolled back and that the car was never flooded or in a wreck.

3. Set the lowest price you can accept for your car if you are selling it on your own and stick to it. Selling your car can be fun if you keep your wits about you!

IF I OWNED A DEALERSHIP...

- I would want both parties to be transparent regarding the trade-in process. Neither party should hold back information.

- I would have an area designated in front of the dealership with an awning and carpeting where you pull in your vehicle if you are thinking about trading.

- A professional would evaluate your car while you are in the dealership and come to you with the offer, and the supporting information for the offer, so the transaction will go faster.

Remember, Ginger Rogers did everything Fred Astaire did, but she did it backwards and in high heels.

~ Unknown

Chapter 6

Negotiating

Negotiation means a discussion intended to produce an agreement. It is also defined as a give and take process between a buyer and a seller in which precise terms of supply and service are agreed. The term also defines a joint process between a buyer and a seller. (Source: Wikipedia)

Flea Markets and Garage Sales

Have you been to a flea market or a garage sale? Have you ever been to a Caribbean island and bargained for a scarf or a T-shirt? My son purchased his wife's diamond engagement ring in Aruba years ago and was able to negotiate quite a difference off the original asking price. (When it was appraised in the United States the diamond was worth more than he paid.) If you don't ask, you'll feel foolish later when you find out someone else did. Let's face it, you are not going to negotiate at an Apple Store for your iPad, or at Nordstrom for a pair of shoes; but you should negotiate for your home, your car and other big ticket items.

Ready – Set – Go

Have your folder or electronic device filled with your research and one of your business cards if applicable. You should know:

- The Manufacturer's Suggested Retail Price (MSRP) also referred to as the window sticker (or Monroney Sticker, named after US Senator Mike Monroney who sponsored the Automobile Information Disclosure Act of 1958)

- The addendum sticker or stickers

- Whether rebates or dealer incentives are available

- Your target price

The MSRP is the manufacturers' assigned price from which the dealers discount the vehicle. The dealer would love for you to pay MSRP, but in today's Internet world, we know this is not the norm unless the model is a special vehicle, in high demand or the hottest car on the market. The Internet price indicates where negotiations will probably start, but it is the dealer's invoice minus holdback plus dealer incentives (this is actually another minus in calculating the dealer's true cost) that determine what is the real vehicle cost to

NEGOTIATING

the dealer. The factory invoice, which is sometimes called the dealer's invoice or dealer's cost, will not appear on the window sticker, but most dealers will show you the vehicle's invoice if you ask. It is from this invoice that you should negotiate. When negotiating, be sure and inquire about any manufacturers' rebates or dealership incentives. Now take the MRSP and multiply it by 2% then take that figure and subtract that from the invoice price. For example, a vehicle with an MRSP of $22,430 X .02 = $448.60. The invoice on this vehicle is $21,373 now subtract the $448.60 which brings the price to $20,924.40 and that is where you start to negotiate. If you've done your Internet research you will have additional data to help you decide where to go from there.

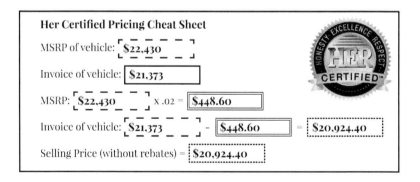

The addendum sticker, which is an additional list attached to the MSRP or Monroney sticker, is worth reading carefully. It should list any items that are added by the dealer after the vehicle is delivered. These items may include paint protection, window tinting, a clear bra or more universal add-ons such as pin-striping, door edge guards, wheel well enhancements, and even rear spoilers.

At this point, your sales associate goes to his or her manager to see if they can accept your offer. You know they probably will come back with a counter offer and you hope they do it quickly. In the meantime, walk around, look at other models, and comparison shop on your Smartphone.

Most likely they may tell you the offer was unacceptable and the best they can do is "this or that" under or over dealer invoice. You can shake hands at this point and call it a deal or negotiate one more time. If they don't meet your expectations, you are free to walk out and go to another dealership.

Once you've negotiated your car price, you now might mention your trade-in. You know what your car is worth from checking local ads and the websites listed in Chapter 5. If the trade-in offer is a good one, say yes. If not, plan to sell it yourself.

WIN WIN WIN

I am a firm believer that in a car deal there needs to be a win, win, and win. That is three wins: the sales associate, the dealership and the customer. I don't expect the person who spent time helping me purchase my car to go home empty-handed that day. As my father taught me, the sales associate needs to make money. I also don't expect the dealership to forego making money to pay for the electric, staff, and lot attendants. And lastly, I do expect a win for the consumer in the form of a fair price for the selected automobile, and hopefully an ongoing relationship between dealership and buyer.

Take Aways

1. Negotiating is give and take and when the final outcome is a triple win, everyone goes home happy!

2. Negotiating a car deal for the best possible price or payment involves preparedness and knowledge. All of the following terms and factors can determine the outcome you want: dealer invoice, manufacturer's invoice, addendums, incentives, and rebates.

3. Having a car to trade in can be an integral part of your negotiating.

IF I OWNED A DEALERSHIP...

- The General Sales Manager or General Manager would do their best to meet and greet the customer before any negotiating begins. It puts a face to the men and women that are running the dealership.

- I would have the MSRP and dealer invoice presented and explained without being asked.

- Give qualified sales associates more power in closing the deal, this will allow the sale to take less time and cut out all the back and forth that most customers dislike.

- Make the negotiating process seamless and transparent at all times.

A woman and her shoes –
it's a beautiful thing.
~ Unknown

Chapter 7

The Finance Department

In 1944, the average price of a new car was $975 and gas was 15 cents per gallon. At these prices, paying in cash was the norm. Fast forward to present day and it is easy to see why financing an auto is now the preferable way to buy a car, and most dealers would agree.

The finance department (F & I, which stands for Finance and Insurance), also referred to as the business office, has always been where the final deal was made. It's been referred to as the point in the transaction where you wave goodbye to your sales consultant, move down the hall and finalize your payment or total cost. What's trending now is what I've been suggesting for years, which is having your sales and finance person be one and the same. If you know what to expect from the finance department, you will not feel intimidated. You have the right to say no to the extensive products, insurance, extended warranties or service contracts that they offer you. You will be able to drive away with the car you love and have the payment you agreed to.

Quick Facts about How Financing Works

- There are many ways to finance a car, with dealer financing being one of the most popular.

- Car dealers are in the business of selling cars, not making loans. It may seem you are financing with the dealership, but you are actually borrowing from one of the dealer's preferred lenders. Dealers do not write loans but rather act as a broker and are compensated by the lending institution. They have a set of lenders they work with. Usually a dealer works primarily with the manufacturer's lender.

- Finance managers should work on your behalf to get you the best financing available.

- A dealer may want to pull a credit report early in the car shopping process (bring yours with you). This is a way for the dealers to evaluate your approval rate on a loan for the car you are interested in.

- Dealers can impact your interest rate. It's legal for them to add a point or two onto the finance company's interest rate and keep the difference as a fee for finding a lender for you. Ask the dealer if he has added points to the rate, if so how many, and then question the reason.

- There are advantages of working with the dealer's lenders, one being convenience, of course. There is a lot to be said for having one stop shopping for your car and financing available in the same place, during the day, night, or weekends. Dealers' finance departments can also offer excellent interest rates and other manufacturer incentives. Finance managers should be happy to pass on incentives and special interest rates; ask in case they didn't mention it. It's all part of your being a savvy consumer.

Know Your Credit Worthiness

If you allow your sales associate to check your credit immediately, which I suggest you <u>don't</u> (see Chapter 2), he or she pulls it up themselves or goes to the finance department to do so. Either way they now know everything about your financial situation such as debt, bankruptcy, divorce etc. This is why you should do your credit check <u>on your own</u>.

That said, dealers will have to pull your credit themselves if you intend to finance with them or write a personal check. Only paying cash will eliminate the dealer from pulling your credit report with the credit bureau.

Remember, when you pull up your credit score, this will not result in a "ding," as it is not an inquiry from a credit institution. When you check your credit score yourself prior to shopping for your car, you can quickly review loan rates at a number of different lenders online.

Bankrate.com is a good place to start, as it is important to know what current rates are available to you.

Your bank or credit union may have given you pre-authorization for a $30,000 car loan and at a rate better than the dealer can offer. You should know all of this prior to going to the dealership. Depending on your credit rating, I have found more often than not, the manufacturer's financial arm has the best interest rates out there; Ford Motor Credit, Chrysler Capital and BMW Financial Services to name a few, however I've found that they have more stringent credit requirements.

I mentioned this earlier, but it bears repeating. It is now a federal law that you need to authorize the pulling of your credit report. Your signature on the credit application is your authorization for the dealership to run a credit report on you.

Can I Super-Size Your Purchase?

In the finance department you are asked if you wish to add on other extra products and services. Please understand the finance department's job is to offer you these products.

However, the first rule in a dealership is "everything is negotiable" and these products have a very large markup and from the dealer's perspective "wiggle room." If you are considering any of these products or services, this is an excellent opportunity to "wiggle" the price down. Also, they may be presented as "it will only add $50 to your monthly payment." It will only add $50 to your monthly payment but never lose sight of the increase; it's still costing you $3,000 plus interest over all.

Here is an overview of some of the types of extended warranties and insurance coverages you may be offered in the finance office and what they include. It's a good idea to know what they are and what they cover before you're faced with them in the finance office.

Manufacturer Warranties and Extended Warranties

Manufacturer warranties are guarantees from the manufacturer that they will repair failures at no cost for a specific length of time or until you reach a certain number of miles, whichever comes first. An extended warranty is the generally accepted term for what is technically a vehicle service contract or mechanical breakdown insurance. An extended warranty is actually a contract between you and the warranty provider that says if you maintain your vehicle properly, they will pay for covered repairs. The important note here is whether it's the manufacturer's warranty or an extended warranty, you are required to perform the manufacture's recommended maintenance procedures or else you will void your coverage.

Manufacturers are required by law to cover certain factory installed parts for defects in materials or workmanship. In the United States all new vehicles come with a basic warranty, also known as bumper to bumper coverage, and some vehicles also include a limited powertrain or drivetrain warranty once the basic warranty expires. Additionally, Federal mandates require manufacturers to cover some emissions equipment for eight years or 80,000 miles, and passive restraint systems for five years or 50,000 miles.

Extended warranties are regulated by your state's Department of Insurance. Some states are more aggressive in their requirements than others. In Florida for example, the retail price of a warranty must be registered with the Department of Insurance and the warranty cannot be sold for any more than the registered retail price. In California, extended warranties are called mechanical breakdown insurance (MBI) and classified as insurance and also price controlled.

A <u>MANUFACTURER'S BASIC WARRANTY</u>, is also known as a "bumper to bumper" warranty. Depending on the vehicle make and model, for new cars this will typically cover from 36 months or 36,000 miles and some manufacturers go up to 60 months or 60,000 miles. The basic warranty covers most components with the exception of standard maintenance and replaceable items, which are subject to wearing out in the normal course of driving. This includes parts such as brake pads, filters, belts, hoses and wiper blades.

Some companies, like BMW, for example, will include a maintenance plan to cover some of the standard maintenance items. This is a separate maintenance plan not part of the warranty. See the owner's manual, dealer, or check the manufacturer's website for the specific warranty coverages that come with your particular vehicle.

If your vehicle also comes with a <u>LIMITED POWERTRAIN WARRANTY</u>, this starts when the basic warranty expires and depending on the manufacturer, can run from 60 months or 60,000 miles up to 120 months or 100,000 miles. The powertrain warranty only covers the engine, transmission, axles and driveshaft. If your engine or transmission stops running, you may think the limited powertrain warranty will cover it, however it only covers the parts inside the engine or transmission. It does not cover most of the major causes of an engine or transmission running poorly or not running at all such as electrical issues, modules, sensors or computers. Powertrain warranties only cover limited catastrophic failures and only for defects in materials or workmanship and not wear and tear, so don't be lulled into a false sense of security.

You can also purchase an <u>EXTENDED WARRANTY</u>

which will extend coverage beyond the original manufacturer's warranty. These are generally the same level of coverage as the manufacturer's warranty with the exception of not covering body components such as paint issues, weather stripping and moldings or glass. They also do not cover interior components such as fabric or carpeting. With a new car, make sure you are purchasing an "exclusionary wrap" extended warranty. Exclusionary means it is the same level of coverage as the original basic warranty, and wrap means it will "wrap" around the manufacturer's warranty and you're not paying for overlapping coverage. Also make sure it will be honored nationwide at any repair facility and not just at the dealership where you purchased it. Before considering an extended warranty, consider how long you intend on keeping your car. If you don't plan on keeping it past the original manufacturer's basic warranty, an extended warranty would be of no value.

Extended Warranties for Used Vehicles

You can purchase an extended warranty for a used vehicle to help defer some of the inevitable repair costs and for peace of mind. There are three types of extended warranties available and the level of coverage you qualify for is dependent on the age and mileage of the vehicle. The coverage types and levels are:

Exclusionary: This is equivalent to the manufacturer's basic warranty and the highest level of coverage you can purchase. This coverage is so extensive the contract will not list any parts covered, only the parts that are not covered or excluded, hence the term exclusionary. Generally available for vehicles up to 6 or 7 years old and under 85,000 miles.

<u>Stated Component</u>: This covers about 60% to 70% of a vehicle and will contain some level of coverage for most major mechanical and electrical components. The contract does list or state the parts covered, hence "stated component." Generally available for vehicles up to 10 years old and under 120,000 miles.

<u>Powertrain:</u> This is the same level of coverage as the manufacture's limited powertrain warranty and only covers about 20% to 30% of your vehicle. This is for catastrophic failures only and should only be purchased if you absolutely must keep your vehicle running for financial reasons. Generally available for vehicles up to 15 years old or under 150,000 miles.

If the value of your car is under $10,000 you may want to avoid an extended warranty. Given the cost of the warranty, your return on investment is questionable.

Extended warranties are available from the dealership, or you may find better pricing from a third party. Do an online search for "extended auto warranty companies." Get a few quotes to compare prices and if you ever feel pressured to buy, you're talking to a company you don't want to do business with. The top providers will not pressure you into purchasing. Remember to always buy the highest level of coverage you qualify for to get the best value for your money. And <u>always</u> read the contract before purchasing.

Certified Pre-Owned Vehicle Warranties

Most manufacturers have a certified pre-owned program where a used vehicle undergoes an inspection by the dealership and is certified to pass as "mechanically sound" and is given a short term warranty of one or two years. The vehicle must be relatively new and have low miles to qualify.

Keep in mind the vehicle was not inspected by the manufacturer but by certified technicians at the dealership. You will be paying a premium for a certified vehicle and in some cases it is less expensive to buy the car uncertified and purchase a longer term extended warranty. Do the numbers.

<u>ROADSIDE ASSISTANCE</u>– Some automakers include roadside assistance with their bumper-to-bumper or powertrain warranties, while others have separate policies. These programs cover anything from flat-tire changes and locksmith services to jump-starts and towing. A few will also reimburse you for incidental costs like meals and motel rooms (if you have to wait for repairs). There are many roadside type plans out there including membership in AAA that you might want to investigate.

<u>TIRES</u>– New car tires are covered by their manufacturer. Depending on the type of tire, most warranties have a year or a mileage limit, whichever comes first. Generally, tires are eligible for warranty replacement if the tread-wear indicators reach a certain number. Don't think you will get a new set of tires unless you meet

the policy's qualifiers. Be sure to have your tires rotated regularly by a dealer or authorized facility. Improper rotation, inflation or balancing can void your warranty (unless a special policy has been purchased). Basic tire warranties don't cover punctures, cuts or collision damage. It also does not cover driving with under or over inflated tires, overloading the tire's- weight limit, use of chains or auto racing.

HYBRID COMPONENTS - Components in the hybrid drivetrain include the high-voltage battery pack along with the hybrid assist motor and all the electrical connections in between. Such components may be expensive to repair or replace, so automakers offer generous warranties: In many cases it is about 8 years and 80,000 to 100,000 miles, whichever comes first. My friend purchased a Ford Escape Hybrid and it had a 3 year – 36,000 mile bumper to bumper warranty, but also an 8 year 100,000 mile warranty on the hybrid components. Plus he is in a "Green State" which mandates that the hybrid warranty is extended (free of charge) to 10 years, 150,000 miles.

THIRD PARTY COMPONENTS - Sometimes equipment not made by the vehicle manufacturer, like a DVD player or wireless headphones for a backseat passenger or battery, carry a dedicated warranty from its manufacturer. Take note, they are likely shorter than the bumper-to-bumper warranty for the car.

Note: *A Consumer Reports survey found that 55% of owners who purchased an extended warranty hadn't used it for repairs during the* *lifetime of the policy, even though the median price paid for the coverage was just over $1,200.00. Others that were surveyed said the extra coverage came in handy and saved them money once they remembered they had purchased it. However, what Consumer Reports didn't take into account in their study is the asset protection feature of an extended warranty. If your engine goes and you don't have $8,000 sitting in your bank account for the repair, you'll own a very expensive hunk of metal you can't drive but are still making payments on. This is the real value of an extended warranty.*

Consider this…

Extended warranties are one item that you can say no to in the F&I department and purchase at a later time. If you've purchased a new car you are already covered for repairs by the manufacturer's warranty and can wait to purchase the extended warranty later. By waiting, it will cost slightly more and if you're not sure how long you will be keeping your car, it's best to put off the purchase. Just remember to buy one before the manufacturer's warranty expires or else it <u>will</u> cost a lot more. Feeling pressure to buy an extended warranty at the time of purchase is one of the sales strategies that give some dealers a bad reputation.

"**GAP INSURANCE**" (Guaranteed Asset Protection) is something you should consider purchasing in the F&I department, and only if you are financing your automobile.

New cars depreciate the fastest in the first two years of ownership and GAP will cover the difference between the value of the vehicle and what you still owe on it in the event the vehicle is stolen or totaled in an accident. Did you put very little down or roll over negative equity from a previous vehicle loan? The less equity (a.k.a. money) you have in the car the more you need GAP insurance! The general rule-of-thumb is if you've put 20% or more down on the financing, you won't need GAP coverage, otherwise it's a good value for your money.

With a leased vehicle, GAP insurance is usually included in your lease payment, and it is <u>negotiable</u>. My friend's son left a Honda dealership with his first car and was hit at a traffic light. They had purchased GAP insurance and he got a new car as a result.

Gap Insurance Example

Consider that you purchased and financed a $60,000 Mercedes-Benz. Seven months later, you get into an accident and your car is totaled.

    Year 1
   $55,000 (loan payoff)
-$50,000 (vehicle value)
    $5,000 (the gap– what you still owe on the loan)
+ $1,000 (insurance deductible)*
    $6,000 (potential out of pocket expenses)
        $0 (amount you owe <u>because you have gap insurance</u>)

*This may vary with different policies

Year 3

$35,000 (loan payoff)

-$40,000 (vehicle value)

$5,000 (positive equity; you no longer need GAP coverage)

GAP is available for anywhere from two years up to seven years of coverage. Buy the term length that matches your negative equity period, usually the first two or three years depending on how much you had put down.

Don't Worry Be Happy

Don't go in to finance thinking you will be tortured and confused. If you know ahead of time what to expect, it can go quickly and with very little stress. Here are a few tips to get through finance easily:

- Don't enter the finance office unless you have researched independent financing or you have recently checked your credit report and investigated what interest rate your bank or credit union offers. Have your folder or device with you; be prepared. As we stated in Chapter 2, credit reports are available from Equifax.com, Experian.com and Transunion.com.
- Don't forget to have your insurance card with you.
- You probably don't need to buy paint protection, fabric guard, rust protection and VIN etching. Now sometimes these things have already been added onto your car. I've asked to have them all removed but you know that can't

happen; however, you can negotiate the cost of these items. I've been advised over the years to negotiate 50% or more off of the add-ons you didn't ask for.
- Make sure if you say yes to something that you know precisely what you've signed up for.
- Hopefully the finance and insurance person will not advise you that you have to buy the extended warranty to qualify for financing or a better rate. <u>It's not true</u>, and it's illegal to infer it.
- In order to get the monthly payment you need, the finance department might suggest extending the years of payment from three to five. Know what you can afford and how long you want to keep the car before you sign. You should already know your numbers.
- Don't sign the contract because you just want to get out of the dealership. Take the time to verify all the essential numbers in the contract. Read, Read, Read. Take your time. Pay particular attention to the <u>Truth in Lending</u> box. The finance manager should go over everything in the Truth in Lending box on the contract before you sign. Nothing in that box should be changed without your initials.
- Separate the price, tax, title and DOC fees so you know the value of each <u>individually</u>. By the way, a male friend of mine thought DOC fees were monies paid at the DOCK in Los Angeles to ship the cars to the dealership. A DOC fee, also

called a document or documentation fee, is a fee charged by car dealerships to process a vehicle's paperwork. Essentially, a DOC fee covers the cost of all the dealership's back-office employees, from the people who handle the money to the employees who deal with the title, registration and the DMV.

Weekend and Holiday Buyers

When an auto deal goes amiss it might be because you purchased your vehicle on a Sunday when the banks are closed. This also is the case when you close on a mortgage, as rates can fluctuate daily. You've been told you have a payment of $270 per month, but on Monday it's $280! It can go the other way as well and your payment might be slightly lower.

For a Sunday or legal holiday deal, you can sign the documents based on the wording "it looks like the payment is…" If the payment turns out to be more than you can handle, you can either sign at the actual new rate or return the car. A sharp salesperson will make this point very clear! This scenario usually applies to credit-challenged customers. When the payment is under, the customer is happy. But when it's over, it is not good for the sales associate or dealer's reputation.

Don't ever be afraid to hold the deal and come back the next day, or when the bank is open and you have a definite rate. I choose to purchase cars during the week, end of month, end of quarter or end of year for the best deal. Unbundle your deal by knowing each and every charge. There is no reason why buying a car needs to be painful or dreaded.

Lease ~ Own ~ Finance

You have choices when it comes to owning a car:

Lease – You are essentially borrowing or "renting" the car for a few years, usually two to three, sometimes five

Own – You purchase the car outright by check or cash for the negotiated price of the car.

Finance of a New or Used Vehicle – You finance your new or used car for a set price and terms and you co-own it with the lending institution.

I've owned cars using all three methods over the years, based on my financial situation at the time, my job, miles driven per year, rebates, and dealer offers. Each one of these options still requires that you do your homework and know where you are in your life, career and future.

Lease Your New Vehicle

Auto leasing is essentially a car rental, but for a longer time period and with some extra fees. Many people prefer leasing to buying because it allows them to drive a new car every few years. It also allows for predictable lifestyle changes that would create the need for a change of vehicle. Remember, an automobile is a depreciating asset, so for some, leasing is the smarter choice.

Note: If a lease vehicle is in an accident and that accident is reported to CARFAX you aren't financially affected. If you purchased the vehicle, and it's been involved in an accident and reported to CARFAX, it lowers the value of your vehicle when you trade or sell it.

Unlike buying, you never own the car (and you have to return it at the end of the lease unless you chose to buy it at that time for the residual amount.) Your monthly payment is based on the car's depreciation (how much the car's value decreases.) So cars that hold their value are actually better for leasing. Also, if you can write off your mileage for your job or business, a lease is very desirable. In the last few years lease terms have been relaxed, making leasing your vehicle something to consider. In addition, there is less financial responsibility when leasing and GAP insurance is usually included by the lender. Depending on your garaging address and the state you live in, sales tax can be less on a lease, and maintenance is usually residualized (as you are usually still under manufacturer's warranty.)

To Lease or Not to Lease, When is Leasing Right for You?

Consider this:

Newlyweds lease a two-seater sports car for 2 years knowing they want to start their family towards the end of their lease period. They finish their lease and decide to purchase a small SUV knowing they will need a child's safety seat adaptation and different cargo space with a family of three. They enjoyed the sports car for a couple of years, and then just returned it to the dealership. They want to <u>own</u> a car that will accommodate their expanding family.

Or this:

A real estate agent friend of mine who shows properties in upscale neighborhoods said that choosing the right vehicle to lease is important. Historically a real estate sales associate would lease a vehicle that could fit at least five passengers who matched their clients' current or higher demographic. This was to visually demonstrate to the client that he or she had been very successful in the industry, thus would be a perfect choice to be their agent.

Over the years, with the depreciation of property and the debacle of lending institutions, many realtors started leasing more practical vehicles. This last year my friend leased a Prius to give the message to his clients that we all care about the environment and that saving on gas gives people more money to "purchase a home." He adjusts his auto lease choices based on the economy and the ever-changing real estate industry.

Some Guidelines for Leasing

Check for Lease Specials – I like to use manufacturers and dealer automotive websites to check out their incentives page. You may see ads on TV and the internet where they might promise 0% financing and lease payments of $220 per month. Remember, there is <u>fine print</u> such as $4,000 down, military discount, AARP discount, former Dallas Cheerleader discount (just kidding), but always read and understand any fine print on the lease ad.

My husband is notorious for seeing an ad on TV and yelling to me from the family room. "Cathy, we can get a new BMW for $269 per month." What he didn't read was the fine print; $5,000 down payment and 7,500 miles per year on approved credit and 72-month lease. You would think after all these years living with me that he would pay more attention to the fine print!!!!!

Now that you have decided to lease, here are a few things to be cognizant of:

- The length of lease in months, 24 to 60
- The amount due at signing (I recommend putting the minimum down)
- The monthly payments including taxes and all fees
- The inclusion of GAP insurance in the contract
- Fees at the end of your lease. Read your lease vehicle agreement carefully, in particular your end-of-lease obligations, including any disposition fees (such as excessive mileage, body damages or tire tread depth deficiencies)
- Once you have signed your lease contract, I suggest you make a commitment to maintain your vehicle even though it is a "rental." Have the maintenance performed at

scheduled intervals to comply with the terms of the lease. Often there are incentives such as free lube and oil included in 24-month leases. The dealer wants you to return a great resale car in two years.

- Make sure you stay within the mileage limits to avoid extra fees at the end of your term. Residuals are based on mileage per year, which can vary. You can pay in advance if you know you might go over the miles for less money per mile than at the end of your lease. If you chose to do that, and don't use the extra miles you purchased, most lease companies will refund any unused miles you purchased up front.

- When you near the end of your lease, you will have to decide the future of your vehicle. Either you can turn the car in, begin another lease or purchase it for the residual amount stated in your contract. If you decide to keep it, make sure you've done all the necessary research to confirm you are making a savvy decision.

Own Your New or Used Vehicle Outright

Use the same research we have discussed. Just because you are lucky enough to pay in cash for your new ride, you still want to get it for the best price! Dealers make money from leasing and financing, not cash, therefore other than the possibility of the process going quicker, it isn't the most desirable for the dealer. Make sure you have negotiated as if you were financing.

Finance Your New or Used Vehicle

If you are going to buy a new or used vehicle from a dealer, make sure, as mentioned before, you have checked all finance options before you arrive. However, more often than not, due to your finances and past history, the dealer may be your best bet for financing, but make sure you know exactly what your options are, and what you can afford.

Auto warranty source courtesy of:

ConsumerAutomotiveResearch.com

For a list of glossary terms regarding warranties go to **HERcertified.com** - Resources

Take Aways

1. You are the one with the final say in the Finance Department - when you know what you can say yes or no to, it's less stressful and confusing.

2. Sometimes manufcturer's financing is your best bet, depending upon your finances and credit history.

3. When considering any warranties it's prudent to understand what is and isn't covered so that you can make an informed decision.

IF I OWNED A DEALERSHIP..

- I would have the sales associate I was matched with and the finance manager be the same person.

- I would insist that the sales associate clearly explain each item that may be offered to the customer before they enter the Finance Department. Maybe a printed check list or menu to physically show the customer.

- Researchers have found that "dark chocolate" can relieve stress. I would have several pieces of dark chocolate readily available in the finance offices, perfect for a customer's sweet tooth with added health benefits.

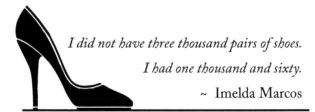

I did not have three thousand pairs of shoes.
I had one thousand and sixty.
~ Imelda Marcos

Remember to read the fine print.

Chapter 8

The Drive Away

You have survived the finance department and hopefully your agreed upon payment didn't fluctuate too much and if it did, you are comfortable with your choices and stayed within your budget. Now it's time to meet with your sales associate to learn more about your car in the Drive Away / Delivery experience, and to discuss your complete satisfaction with the car-buying process.

CSI – No, Not the Cop Show

Following the purchase of your new vehicle you will receive a Customer Sales and Service Satisfaction Index (CSI) form. The manufacturer will send you their form via email. This is the report card for the dealership and sales associate. Please complete the CSI scorecard and return to the manufacturer. This is the manufacturer's way of measuring your overall experience, and understanding how you feel about the car buying process in which you just participated. A "completely satisfied" in each category is very important to the sales associate, so most sales associates go out of their way to make sure your experience is a good one. You should not receive any kind of incentive from your salesperson or the dealership to entice you to fill out the CSI form. I also think it is unprofessional, as do most new car customers, if the dealership is continually asking that you give them a high CSI score. A 100% CSI score should be earned by the dealership, not begged or badgered. The manufacturer notifies the dealership of a poor or excellent CSI score upon receipt of the survey.

I always complete and email the form as I feel the dealership deserves the courtesy of rating their service. Whether you fill it out with a good or unsatisfactory ratings, I believe you should score your experience. If you are thinking of submitting a poor rating, ask yourself, did you make the dealership aware of your issue(s), and did they respond to your feedback. I believe it is only fair if you have problems and/or questions, you should professionally make the dealership aware during the process. A good sales associate and staff will work with you. Feel free to let them know throughout the process if something is bothering you or how you want the process to proceed. Don't wait to give them a bad ranking without making them aware of any areas in which you are not satisfied.

Delivery and Learning Curve

Next you will take delivery of your new car with your sales associate, and possibly a product expert if the manufacturer of your vehicle has implemented specific customer product support. Most of the premium brand manufacturers have taken the additional step of providing dedicated individuals to help the customer learn about their vehicle. These individuals typically have no sales responsibility, and are 100% dedicated to serve the customer.

You should expect to spend at least 45 minutes with your salesperson or designated product expert so they can thoroughly go over the car with you and answer all your questions. This will include everything from the basics like where is the fuel, hood, and trunk release, to helping you set the audio, showing you how the vehicle's navigation system works, to downloading your Smartphone's contacts and music.

The individual is there to help you and you should feel comfortable asking as many questions as you need in order for you to understand the many advanced features contained in today's vehicles.

The person doing your delivery should offer their business card and encourage you to call or text them should you have any questions as you begin driving and becoming more familiar with your new vehicle. As dealerships and manufacturers are now focusing more and more on customer service, many dealers will now offer to have you schedule a follow-up appointment either at the dealership, your office, or your home to further help familiarize you with your new vehicle.

Before you leave the dealership, your sales associate should take you to the service department and explain how it operates. They should also give you a business card from both the service manager and the person you would like to be your service advisor. It is important for you to have these contacts as the service department should really strive to make you happy whenever you need to take your vehicle in for service.

Now may be a good time to reflect on your experience of buying a new or used car. Was it worth all the effort of researching for the right vehicle, choosing your sales associate, negotiating from a place of knowledge and being confident in making the right decision? You should feel good about what you've accomplished and especially the price you paid.

I've probably leased, bought and financed forty cars or more either for myself or others. Goodness knows I've test driven over 500. I've always suggested folks celebrate the purchase of a car so it becomes a part of the adventure. I would call my father and tell him what I bought and why, the color, and how much I paid. I always let him know it was because of him that I was able to make the best deal. Our tradition was ice cream cones as we drove home in a new car... What is yours?

You see, half the fun is knowing what you are doing and being able to tell people what a great experience you had. Maybe you want to write a review of your first test drive or your first month owning the car. Many automotive websites welcome reviews from owners. Actually, those reviews can garner as much attention as the ones I write, where the manufacturer has asked me to test drive one of their new models.

Take Aways

1. Positive customer reviews are necessary for the dealership and sales associate to attain an excellent "Report Card" from the manufacturer. They should bend over backwards to accommodate your expectations for a good experience. Speak up if something is not going the way you would like.

2. Take the necessary time to learn about your new car, from trunk-popping to technology!

3. Celebrate your car purchase with someone who cares.

IF I OWNED A DEALERSHIP...

- The delivery of the vehicle, new or pre-owned, would be presented in a separate red carpet area at the dealership. The delivery area would include the car parked in front of a scenic backdrop that the client chooses. Photos would be taken of the client with their car in front of a beach, mountains, golf course, etc.

- Each customer would be presented with a gift card to purchase an item from the dealership's accessories department. The value of the gift card would be based on the selling price of the vehicle purchased.

- Personal follow up and thank you cards would be sent to ensure that the customer feels appreciated.

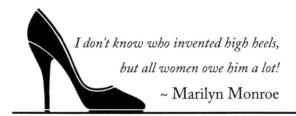

I don't know who invented high heels, but all women owe him a lot!
~ Marilyn Monroe

Chapter 9

Service

To me, the word service means "customer service" whether it involves a server in a restaurant, a shoe department sales associate, or a business I frequent to have something fixed or completed that I can't do myself. Hair salons, tire stores, or even the concierges at hotels can be "customer service" providers.

The repair and maintenance of your vehicle is a service we pay dearly for and we should expect the same respect and exceptional service as we do from Nordstrom.

Automotive Service Department

According to the Automotive Aftermarket Industry Association, nine out of ten women are involved in their household's vehicle maintenance and repair decision-making process. Industry experts say 65-70% of the customers taking cars in for service are women.

My mother would carry a grocery list of items my dad gave her to rattle off to the service department. I don't remember her ever looking at the list. Let me tell you, my mother could imitate the sound coming from under the hood or describe a smell and color of any unusual drips to the service department with great detail.

"I smell an odor much like burning rubber in a car fire on a hot humid day on a Florida morning." Or "I found a puddle of liquid under the car that was half yellow and half green that shimmered like the gills of tropical fish."

Interesting ... the mechanic usually knew what it was right away.

Many service writers tell me they like to talk to women about what is wrong with cars. Men tend to come in and tell the service writers and mechanics what's wrong with their vehicle rather than explaining the problem. I once heard a male service writer say to a doctor, "Sir, if I came to you with stomach pain and walked into your office telling you I have to have my appendix out, what would you say? First you would want me to describe my symptoms in detail and ask more questions to find out exactly what is wrong. Well, that is how we like to handle automotive problems. Tell us what you are experiencing, describe the problem as best you can, and we will examine and determine the problem."

Hopefully you will feel confident and comfortable at the service department of the dealership where you purchased your vehicle. You probably recall that I suggested you tour the service area to check for cleanliness both of the service facilities, and the grooming of the service writers as part of searching for your ideal car dealership. I also suggest you find out if loaner cars are issued, if your repair or maintenance needs are extended beyond your work day or deadline. Usually when your service needs are less than a day, a shuttle is provided to get you to your destination. Maybe you even picked up a service advisor's card during your personal delivery tour so you have a name and are ahead of the game. Just like choosing your sales associate, you might like to work with another service advisor on staff that day, just ask ... no hard feelings. If you don't want to say anything to that person, just ask for the service department director and discuss it with him or her.

Money Money Money

The service department of a dealership is a finely-tuned machine that produces significant revenue for the dealership. Statistically, a woman will drive her vehicle up to the service advisor's window at least two or three times a year. We may be there for routine maintenance, an item under warranty, a recall, or repairs needed on an older or out of warranty vehicle.

Have you ever taken your vehicle in for service and while you are sitting in your car, stretching your legs, and waiting for your service advisor, a sales associate approaches you out of the blue? The conversation might start off with "what a nice day it is" or "how old is your car?" or even "have you thought of trading this in for a new car, we have 0% down financing this month?" This is a subtle way of hopefully interesting you in a new car or truck.

Most women I've surveyed do not like this approach as they are already a little anxious waiting to hear about their car's repairs and the anticipated bill. However, there are times when you've had enough repairs done that are costing you more than a lease payment, and at that time you might welcome some conversation as to the possibilities. If you are interested, ask for their card and call them when it's convenient for you.

Customer retention is NO. 1 for dealerships. The more a customer comes back to the dealership where they purchased their car, the higher the likelihood they will not only return for service in the future, but will also purchase their next car from the dealership. A dealer would like you to let them know if you are not happy with your service writer so they can quickly assign you to a new one, or the service director may take care of you personally. An unsatisfied customer in the dealership service department is unacceptable. The automotive retail business is so competitive, a good dealership cannot afford to have even one unsatisfied customer telling others, either in person or online, that they were not happy with the service.

What is a Service Advisor or Service Writer?

The first person you should encounter when you pull into the service area of your dealership is the Service Advisor or Writer (same thing) or a customer service concierge to direct you. They are not mechanics or technicians; they are in many ways a sales associate. Most service writers are paid on commission, so the more work you have done, the more money they make.

This does not mean they suggest you have work done you don't need, but many times they make useful suggestions such as "While you are here, let's make sure everything that is serviced under warranty can be done at the same time." or "You are due for an oil change in a month; let's do it now so you won't need to come back."

Note: You may have received a year's worth of oil and lube that needs to be done at the dealership where you purchased the vehicle. This is very smart gift from the dealer, as it keeps the customer coming back to the same dealership.

Read your owner's manual. The manufacturer might say you need an oil change every six months or 7,500 miles, yet your service advisor might suggest the "dealer recommended service or maintenance." This might be every three months or 3,500 miles. I would follow the manufacturer's recommended time frame.

This is not to suggest you let things go. After all, the better you maintain your vehicle the longer you will have it. It is especially important to take care of your lease vehicle, as excessive damage, abuse and neglect can be charged back to you at the end.

How the Process Should Work

A written estimate is a contract between you and the shop. It describes what service needs to be done and how much it will cost. Even if your state does not require written estimates, insist on one.

I like to see the hourly rate of labor listed separately. Rates vary across the country anywhere between $80 and $140 an hour depending on the make and model and facility doing the work. If under warranty, the labor and parts are at no charge.

Sometimes you will sign for a particular repair but when they get under the hood they may find more problems. After all, technicians use computers to diagnose problems and once they get going, you just don't know what they might find.

If fixing the next series of problems requires more time and money, they should get in touch with the service customer (you) in order to approve additional work. To make sure this is done in a timely manner you might want to allow texting or emailing as a way to improve the efficiency of communications.

Make sure you know what is covered under your dealer warranty or extended warranty. Many times the covered repair needs to be pre-authorized by the warranty company or they can deny payment.

When your car is ready for pick up you should be notified by phone, text, or email if that is what you requested. Make sure you have communicated with your service advisor so there is no misunderstanding. The dealership service department would like an excellent rating when asked to score their report card. Just like the CSI survey you receive when buying a new car, the service area has the same rating system. It is important that you have communicated what you expect, need and want.

Interesting New Data

There is manufacturer data showing that many brands of vehicles have wonderful service, based on the "culture" of the individual dealership. Hopefully, that is where you purchased your vehicle.

Check out These Facts

1. 73% of women said they intend to service their car at the dealership where they purchased their vehicle.

2. 53% said they always have their car service work completed at the same dealership where they purchased their car.

3. 66% of the women received follow-up communication from the dealership after the work was completed.

4. Dealerships that understand the importance of customer satisfaction for their women customers will go out of their way to have a percentage of their service writers be women, as it is a known fact that women generally have a higher trust of other women.

What Do I Do if My Car is Recalled?

A recall occurs when a manufacturer (or NHTSA – National Highway Traffic Safety Administration) determines that a car model has a safety-related defect or does not comply with a federal safety standard. When this occurs, the automaker will alert owners to the problem and offer to repair the defect for free. Don't think you are getting a new car. They will fix or replace the recall item; rarely do they replace the vehicle.

Car companies are required to send letters to customers affected by a recall. You can also stay up-to-date on recalls by visiting NHTSA's website.

The recall letter should contain the following information:
- A description of the defect.
- The risk, hazard or potential injuries that may occur.
- How the manufacturer plans to fix the problem, including when the parts will be available and how long it may take.
- Instructions on what to do next. Generally you'll be instructed to call your local dealer to set up a repair appointment.

FYI – If you have a tire recall you must have it done within sixty days of receiving the notification. Go to SaferCar.gov for more information.

A safety recall does not mean you are in immediate danger; however, if you learn that your car has been recalled, it's best not to take the risk. Have your car repaired as soon as possible, especially if the defect could pose a major hazard. You do not pay to have your car fixed on a recall. You will need to take your car to an authorized dealer since they contract directly with the manufacturer. I suggest you bring your recall letter with you. The dealer should not charge you. If he does, ask to see the manager. Bear in mind that recalls might not start being serviced for 30 to 60 days due to parts availability.

Whether you are bringing your car in for repairs, having warranty work done, or complying with a recall notice, the service department will take care of you. Customer service is just that, pleasing the customer. Sometimes it involves taking suggestions from customers to improve the service. Each time a customer feels something is missing in the process, a new idea or effort is put into play. New ideas were put into practice the first time a man or woman said to a service writer, "I could use a cup of coffee" or "Is there somewhere I can work on my paper work or entertain my children and maybe watch the news?"

I've been to dealerships and other auto facilities that take customer service to a whole new level with custom changing tables for babies, including diapers and wet wipes. Some facilities have latte machines and full-on cafés for food and coffee. When a facility takes customer service to a new level I know they understand today's customer's needs, and female's needs in particular.

When I personally check-out dealerships, I expect the customer service standards to be equal whether it's Kia or Jaguar. We all want to be treated like we are special whether we purchased a $15,000 or $150,000 car. It is also important that as customers, we handle ourselves with the same dignity we expect from our automotive professionals.

I say "treat people the way you want to be treated, and I want to be treated with respect."

Take Aways

1. The service department's customer service is crucial to the overall success of the dealership. Don't be shy when explaining your car troubles, or asking for a shuttle, a loaner car, or a quiet place to do your work while you wait.

2. Make sure you have a written estimate of the work to be completed, a clear understanding of what needs to be done, and whether it is covered under warranty.

3. Make sure your contact information is up-to-date for recall notifications or service reminders.

IF I OWNED A DEALERSHIP…

- I would provide shuttle service or offer loaner cars, Wi-Fi, beverage and snacks, and quiet work stations for the customers to work while their cars are being serviced. I would have the service advisors frequently keep in touch with their customers via text.
- I would have the service department manager check the data base whenever a recall notification is issued for a specific model. Although it is not the dealership's responsibility, it's good customer service to verify that the car owner is aware of the recall, and schedule an appointment.
- Efficiency and quality in the service area are essential for repeat business and profit. Always ensure that the customer knows you value their time. Keep them informed of their vehicle's progress while it is in the service department. A follow-up thank you note is great for letting the customer know a dealership genuinely cares about them and their business.
- Greet every service customer with a kind word, and a warm smile…

65-70% of service customers are women

Keep your heels, head, and standards high!
~ Unknown

Chapter 10

Some Final Thoughts

The purpose of writing this guide for women was to bring awareness to women and the auto dealers alike about the selling methods women prefer. After all, I've worked for dealerships that allowed me to advertise and market in ways that women would not find intimidating. I've led sales training classes, done mystery shopping, and attended dealer and manufacturer meetings to encourage new modes of connecting with women in the dealership sales process.

I've designed the **HER Certified**™ program based on research, knowledge, and self-confidence.

What Women Want in a HER Certified™ Experience!

Honesty

Excellence

Respect

Transparency

Business Relationship Built on Trust

Amenities to Fit their Needs

A Good Deal

Driving in Your New Car with High Heels

I've been wearing high heels since I was granted permission by "Vinny and Ruth" which was when I was about sixteen years old. I realized that my desire was to look and feel taller than my 5'2 stature. It was also to emulate my mother, who was 4'11 and who wore them till she was in her eighties.

I've jumped rope in heels, played hop scotch, cooked dinner, raced cars, worn with short shorts in the 70's and danced to John Travolta's "Stayin' Alive" during the same era. I was careful not to walk a boardwalk or anything with planks or separations as my heel would always get stuck in-between and scratch up the colored part making them look scuffed up. I worked hard to save enough money for a moderately priced, well-fitting shoe; I didn't want to ruin them. My shoes were my one and only accessory for many years. They were the accessory that made me feel tall and confident.

SOME FINAL THOUGHTS

Care an Maintenance of Our Heels

I switch shoes for driving. I have a pair of sturdy flats that I keep in the car in a tote bag, worn just for that reason. I place my high heels in the bag and drive with flats. When I arrive at my destination, where I want to wear heels, I switch them out. Remember, as you accelerate and brake, the back of the heel of your shoe will show wear and tear and ruin your heels over a period of time. I do test drive cars with manual transmission and that really beats up your heels. This rule is true for all size heels whether platforms or two-inch heels.

Not every woman can wear heels, nor do they choose to. Some women wear heels so high they can barely walk and other women feel high heels are torture chambers designed by men. However you feel about your shoe choice, high heels are my metaphor for fairness and self-confidence.

If you can successfully negotiate a car purchase, you can negotiate anything in your life.

IF I OWNED A DEALERSHIP…

- Every woman would leave with a shoe bag with the name of the dealership on the bag and a gift card inside for a pair of shoes.

- I would also have a coupon for FREE oil and lube at the service department of the dealership.

So stand up for what you believe in no matter what shoes you're wearing, high heels just help you stand a little higher.

~ Cathy Droz

Favorite Quotes by My Parents

You don't need college; just read the sports section every day, take a Dale Carnegie course, get your bangs out of your face, and wear high heels, you'll be a success.

~ Vinny Hoffmann 1968

Every woman should own a red pair of high heels ... let your shoes set the tone, after that you open your mouth.

~ Ruth Hoffmann 1967

Automotive journalist, author, speaker, radio host…

About the Author

Cathy Droz is a New York native who loves the automobile industry. At the tender age of seventeen she purchased the family sedan, eventually opening an automotive ad agency in Phoenix, Arizona in her forties. Although Cathy can't fix your car, she can provide expert lifestyle advice on purchasing a vehicle, finding a reputable dealership, choosing an auto repair facility and test-driving a car. Most of all she can tell you what women want in a car buying experience. She is the founder of **HER Certified**™ and she has test-driven over 500 vehicles, giving her insight and knowledge on virtually every make and model on the market.

While the automotive industry makes up a huge part of her life in the workforce, it is just one facet of a manifold career that spans forty-five years. Between both salaried and volunteer positions her titles have included: president of a full service automotive ad agency, travel agent; project manager, copywriter, commercial actress, spokesperson for Perrier water, trade show consultant, account executive; and radio host.

Cathy has led the following organizations: she is the former President of the Phoenix Automotive Press Association, and is a past President and current executive board member of Silent Witness. Her volunteer work includes; PR Director for the Retired NFL AZ Legends, and she has also served with The Harp Foundation, Starshine Academy, and the Young Reporters radio show. She is a member of the Worldwide Who's Who of entrepreneurs and empowers women with her humorous and inspiring speaking engagements. She admits one of her most bizarre experiences was working with the United Professional Wrestling (UPW) organization when she stood in front of 10,000 wrestling fans suggesting they make it family-friendly and was booed out of the ring.

The sum of this varied experience has prepared her for her newest adventure – bridging the gap between women consumers and car dealerships. Her goal is educating the car industry regarding what women want in a car buying experience…Honesty, Excellence in customer service, and most importantly Respect.

Cathy resides in Phoenix, Arizona with her husband Manny. She is the proud parent of three children and nine grandchildren.

Acknowledgments

This book is an accumulation of 20 years in the automotive industry. During those years I acquired opportunities and made long lasting friendships with auto dealers, auto manufacturers, journalists, public relations firms, the media, and customers.

No matter what turn I took in the industry I was blessed with mentors and cheerleaders, both men and women. I would like to take this time to thank those that even once said "I believe in you" or "you go girl."

Thank You.

    Bob Hoffmann – Thanks, Big Brother, for always letting me be part of your automotive world and life. Thank you for pushing me to reach my goals of fair treatment of women. Funny! Who would have thought I'd write a book around our dad's negotiating?

Manny Droz – You have the patience of a saint. You support me in whatever I choose to do, laugh at my jokes, pay the bills, change grandbaby's dirty diapers, and you married me twice. Talk about confident!

To My Three Children – Jason Droz, Julia Serafine and Melanie Shawcroft – Thank you for being so supportive, loving and fun to be around. Thank you, Kacey Droz, Damian Serafine and Matt Shawcroft who call me Mom and my beautiful grandchildren: Jayden, Hudson, Greyson, CrosbyVincent Droz, Sofia, Gabriella, Ava Serafine, Berrett, Spencer Shawcroft, I am enamored with each and every one of you.

In No Particular Order – Thank You

Alan Mulally, Tom Keegan, Bill Hughes, Carol-Ann Hoffmann, Larry Edsall, Linda Williams, Carrie Owens, Jodie Wilson, Ian Percy, Barry Kluger, Jason Ake, Knox Ramsey, Jim Seemiller, Jim Atkinson, Tim Richards, Steve Fusco, Lea Haben Woodford, Wally Cahill, Jan DiAtri, Pete and Kati Walker, Cynthia Richmond, David Kimmerle, Robert Merlin Davis, Tony Perlongo, Tony Komadina, Autumn Henderson, Ed Zito, Becky Antioco, Cathy Luebke and the Press Association, Casey Weber, Sheilah Dancer, Coye Pointer, Annette Loertscher, Cindy Kelly, Lincoln Kennedy, Brian Smith, Jane and Ben Gordon, Karen DeWall, Deborah Bateman, John Vaccaro, Paul Webb,

ACKNOWLEDGMENTS

Art Coleman, Christian Gomez, Amy and Nick Wittenrood, Tony Pennacchio, Neil Schrock, John and Jim Testa, Dave Zoloto, Iza Shewan, Nick Vincelli, Mario Andretti, Lyn St. James, Eboni Lacey, Rick McPartlin, Stephanie Jarnagan, Steve Bowers, Tom Irwin, Silvianne Gonsalves, Bill "Z," Bob Fishman, Patti and Howard Fleischmann-Community Tire, Ben Smith.

Acknowledgments for the Book

Cathy Burford – Editor – Project Manager – Not just my editor but my friend for more than 25 years. You never make fun of my spelling, punctuation or vocabulary, you just make it sound right. When doors open you tell me to run through and when doors close you encourage me to try another door. You give and give of your time and resources without wanting anything in return. Thank you for adding commas to my run on sentences and tolerating my run on mouth.

Deborah Brown – Publisher – I remember the day you said… don't worry I will "breathe" into your book and make it something you will be proud of. You told me to empower women first and foremost by building their confidence through car buying. Thank you for your patience and encouragement.

Editor: Cathy Burford – Deborah Brown
Photography – Kacey Droz – AboutLoveStudio.com
Models – Jackie Mahaney, Robin Leggio, Jayden Droz, Diesel

Front Cover Team – Graphic Artist: Michael Tierney, Robert Merlin Davis, Scott Hoffmann, Deborah Bateman, Steve Bowers

Technical Advisors – Steve Bowers – Amy Wittenrood

Website and IT Director – Cynthia Sassi

Photo location courtesy of Coulter Infiniti, Mesa, AZ

A special thank you to my mother Ruth Hoffmann who passed away at age 97 while I was finishing this book. Thanks for letting me read you chapters of the book like bedtime stories. I know all you wanted to do was close your eyes, but instead you kept smiling and holding my hand making me feel I could make a difference. This book is for you !!!!!!

God Speed, Dad -

You made it to 99 years of age! You inspired me to write this book through the many lessons that you taught me in business and life. The last thing you said to me was..."Stop talking and make some money." I hope there are plenty of ice cream cones in heaven…

He Said, She Said... What people are saying about
A Woman's Guide to Buying a Car with Confidence and Street Smarts

"Heads up ladies, this book is a 'must buy manual' for car buying gals all around the world. Cathy's no nonsense style reconfirms the purchasing reality that women are beautifully and incredibly different than men, from buying their cars to driving them. Trust me, I know!"

~ **PAT BONDURANT**, President Bondurant Racing School

"First and foremost, *A Woman's Guide to Buying a Car* is a fun and engaging story. Cathy Droz has truly mastered the ability to share her story, with compelling headlines intertwined with accurate and worthwhile facts and data, and an emotional appeal that is relatable and empowering. Auto dealers and salesmen be warned! *A Woman's Guide to Buying a Car* is a 'must' read for anyone embarking on the purchase of a car!"

~ **DEBORAH BATEMAN,** Vice Chairman, National Bank of Arizona

"Cathy Droz was born to write this book. From her childhood stories about tagging along while her father shopped for cars, to her adult jobs working with car dealers, she's gathered valuable nuggets that can help anyone on an automotive shopping adventure. Everyone shopping for a car (man or woman) should study her book before they hit the showroom floor."

   Rick DeBRUHL, ESPN and Velocity Broadcaster

"HER Certified™ sales training hits the sweet spot for educating auto sales people on how to increase sales volume with female clients."

   ~ **TOM HOPKINS**, Tom Hopkins International™

"Buying a car can be a daunting experience even for a 6'6 guy like me. Cathy's book takes the guess work and anxiety out of buying a car. Her humor and street smarts attitude makes this a must read before stepping inside a car dealership."

   ~ **LINCOLN KENNEDY**, Retired NFL –
   Color Commentator Oakland Raiders

"As a HER Certified™ dealer, we've distributed this book to female customers to let them know that we align ourselves with Cathy's beliefs and her process on how to treat women. We have sold more cars to women because of this book and our commitment to HER Certified."

~ **TONY P.**, General Manager, Coulter Infiniti – Mesa, Arizona

"*A Woman's Guide to Buying a Car with Confidence and Street Smarts* is an engaging, entertaining and empowering book. Cathy understands 'what women want' in a car-buying experience and how they want to be treated. The book will save you time and money, whether you are a first time buyer or seasoned car owner. You might even start wearing red high heels."

~ **LEA HABEN WOODFORD,** Author and Publisher of SmartFem.com

Notes